AF405321

A Book Of

ORGANIZATIONAL BEHAVIOUR AND HUMAN RESOURCE MANAGEMENT

BBA (Computer Application)
(Semester - II) : Course Code 201 - Credit 03

(CBCS Pattern 2019)

As Per New Syllabus, Effective from June 2019

Gauri Girish Jadhav
M.Com., MBA - M.Phil., Diploma in Russian Language
Shri Siddhivinayak College of Arts, Commerce and Science,
Pune

NIRALI PRAKASHAN
ADVANCEMENT OF KNOWLEDGE

N4941

Organizational Behaviour & Human Resource Management　　ISBN 978-93-89825-37-4

First Edition　　　：　　January 2020
©　　　　　　　　　：　　Author

Published By:
NIRALI PRAKASHAN
Abhyudaya Pragati, 1312, Shivaji Nagar
Off J.M. Road, PUNE – 411005
Tel - (020) 25512336/37/39, Fax - (020) 25511379
Email : niralipune@pragationline.com

➢ **DISTRIBUTION CENTRES**

PUNE

Nirali Prakashan ： 119, Budhwar Peth, Jogeshwari Mandir Lane, Pune 411002,
(For orders within Pune)　Maharashtra, Tel : (020) 2445 2044, Mobile : 9657703145
　Email : niralilocal@pragationline.com

Nirali Prakashan ： S. No. 28/27, Dhayari, Near Asian College Pune 411041
(For orders outside Pune)　Tel : (020) 24690204; Mobile : 9657703143
　Email : bookorder@pragationline.com

MUMBAI

Nirali Prakashan ： 385, S.V.P. Road, Rasdhara Co-op. Hsg. Society Ltd.,
　Girgaum, Mumbai 400004, Maharashtra;
　Mobile : 9320129587 Tel : (022) 2385 6339 / 2386 9976,
　Fax : (022) 2386 9976
　Email : niralimumbai@pragationline.com

➢ **DISTRIBUTION BRANCHES**

JALGAON

Nirali Prakashan ： 34, V. V. Golani Market, Navi Peth, Jalgaon 425001,
　Maharashtra, Tel : (0257) 222 0395, Mob : 94234 91860;
　Email : niralijalgaon@pragationline.com

KOLHAPUR

Nirali Prakashan ： New Mahadvar Road, Kedar Plaza, 1st Floor Opp. IDBI Bank,
　Kolhapur 416 012, Maharashtra. Mob : 9850046155;
　Email : niralikolhapur@pragationline.com

NAGPUR

Nirali Prakashan ： Above Maratha Mandir, Shop No. 3, First Floor,
　Rani Jhanshi Square, Sitabuldi, Nagpur 440012, Maharashtra
　Tel : (0712) 254 7129;
　Email : niralinagpur@pragationline.com

DELHI

Nirali Prakashan ： 4593/15, Basement, Agarwal Lane, Ansari Road, Daryaganj
　Near Times of India Building, New Delhi 110002
　Mob : 08505972553, Email : niralidelhi@pragationline.com

BENGALURU

Nirali Prakashan ： Maitri Ground Floor, Jaya Apartments, No. 99, 6th Cross,
　6th Main, Malleswaram, Bengaluru 560003, Karnataka;
　Mob : 9449043034
　Email: niralibangalore@pragationline.com

Other Branches : Hyderabad, Chennai

niralipune@pragationline.com　|　www.pragationline.com

Also find us on 🇫 www.facebook.com/niralibooks

Preface ...

It gives us an immense pleasure to present this book on 'Organizational Behaviour and Human Resource Management' for BBA (CA) Semester II students, which covers the several aspects of a Human Resources. All the aspects of human resources are explained in a very simple language

I are extremely grateful to Mr. Jignesh Furia for presenting us with this opportunity.

I would like to thank Mr. Amol Mahabal for putting together the myriad sections in this book and thereby, presenting this book in a systematic way.

I would also like to thank Mr. Ilyas Shaikh, and Mr. Prasad Chintakindi, Mrs. Anjali Muley for their valuable help in preparation of this book.

Suggestions for improvement of this book are always welcome.

AUTHOR

Syllabus ...

Organizational Behaviour and Human Resource Management : BBA (CA) (Sem-II) Course Code 201

1. Introduction to Organizational Behaviour

Definition, Concept, Scope, Models of OB

Major Trends in OB : Total Quality Management, Cultural Diversity, Organizational Change, Stress Management, Sources of Stress, Effects of Stress and Stress Management, Work life Balance and Quality of Work Life.

2. Introduction to HRM

Definition, Concepts, Scope, Importance, Functions, Objectives and Limitations

Role of HR Manager, Areas in which Human Resource Manager can be of Assistance

3. Procurement

HRP – Concept, Definition, Merits and Demerits, Process, Influencing Factors of HRP

Recruitment – Concept, Definition, Sources of Recruitment and Their Utility in Identifying Vacancies, Methods, E- Recruitment

Selection – Concepts, Definition, Process, Types of Interviews and Frequently Asked Interview Questions to the Candidate at Each Step and How to Answer them, E-Selection

4. Training and Development

Concept, Definition, Importance, Methods

E-Training, Recent Trends in Training

☜ ☜ ☜

Contents ...

1. **Introduction to Organization Behaviour** 1.1 - 1.50

2. **Introduction to Human Resource Management** 2.1 - 2.26

3. **Procurement** 3.1 - 3.36

4. **Training and Development** 4.1 - 4.24

    Model Question Paper P.1 - P.2

Chapter 1...

Introduction to Organisational Behaviour

Contents...

1.1 Meaning, Definitions, Scope of Organisational Behaviour
    1.1.1 Features of OB
1.2 Disciplines Contributing to Organisational Behaviour
1.3 Emerging Trends in Organisational Behaviour
1.4 Challenges and Opportunities for Organisational Behaviour
1.5 Organisational Behaviour across Culture
1.6 Models and Approaches of Organisational Behaviour
    1.6.1 OB Models
    1.6.2 Approaches to OB
1.7 Importance of Organisational Behaviour
    1.7.1 Limitations of Organisational Behaviour
1.8 Organisational Change
    1.8.1 Meaning of Organisational Change
    1.8.2 Nature of Organisational Change
    1.8.3 Levels of Change
    1.8.4 Types of Change
    1.8.5 Resistance to Change
    1.8.6 Kurt Lewin's Force Field Analysis Change Model
1.9 Stress Management
    1.9.1 Definitions of Stress
    1.9.2 Sources of Stress
    1.9.3 Effects of Stress
    1.9.4 Stress Management at Workplace
1.10 Work Life Balance
1.11 Quality of Work Life (QWL)
1.12 Total Quality of Management
1.13 Cultural Diversity
    • Points to Remember
    • Questions for Discussion
    • Multiple Choice Questions
    • Project Questions
    • Case Study
    • Questions for Discussion

Learning Objectives ...

- To understand the Meaning and Scope of OB
- To know the Contributions of various disciplines to OB
- To study the Challenges and Opportunities offered by OB
- To understand different Models and Approaches of OB
- To study the Meaning of Organisational Change, its Levels and Types
- To understand the Reasons for Resistance to Change and How to Overcome them
- To know what is meant by Organisational Development, its Objectives and Reasons to study it

---

 **1.1 MEANING, DEFINITIONS, SCOPE OF ORGANISATIONAL BEHAVIOUR**

People often come together to form groups as human nature is gregarious. These groups are formed by people to collectively perform activities of common interest. Organisational behaviour (OB) is the area of study which focuses on human beings and their interaction with other groups and individuals within the organisation. It deals with the study of how people interact within groups, the attitudes of people and groups towards each other and towards the organisation as a whole and its effect on the organisation's functioning and performance. Normally this study is applied to create more efficient business organisations. The central idea of the study of organisational behaviour is to provide a scientific approach to the management of workers.

Definitions of Organisational Behaviour

1. **Luthans:** *"Organisational behaviour is directly concerned with the understanding, predicting and controlling of human behaviour in organisations."*
2. **Stephen Robbins:** *"OB is a systematic study of the actions and attitudes that people exhibit within organisations."*
3. **L. M. Prasad:** *"The study and application of knowledge about human behaviour related to other elements of an organisation such as Structure, Technology and Social Systems."*

Thus Organisational Behaviour is a field of study that analyses the impact that individuals, groups and structure have on behaviour within organisations, so that such knowledge can be used for improving the organisation's effectiveness.

Scope

The role of a manager is becoming crucial as the business environment is constantly changing and the workload and the responsibilities are also increasing.

In an organisation, OB is considered important for various reasons. OB helps to understand the impact of changes in the external environment on an organisation. It also helps organisations to understand its employees better. If employees are satisfied they give their best output, thereby resulting in a more efficient and stable organisation.

Within the HR context, the study of OB and related theories is undertaken to obtain maximum output from individual group members. It can be used to understand attitudes and behaviours of workers and to find out ways to manage them effectively. The study of OB is helpful to explain factors that affect the managerial work and perspectives on the human angle of management. Thus, it helps managers to improve work related understanding of themselves and also of their subordinates.

1.1.1 Features of OB

The following are the Features of OB:

1. **OB is multidisciplinary in nature:** The field is multidisciplinary in nature. It draws heavily from a variety of social science disciplines.

   The study of OB considers the orientation of psychology, to understand the human mind and therefore, behaviour and sociology, to understand the role of an individual in an organisation, as a member of the organisation group, its diversity of ideas, culture, food, language, its ideas, and values.

2. **OB attempts to improve organisational effectiveness and the quality of life at work:** In earlier times, the people as employees in companies were assumed and considered to be lazy who disliked work, and if given the choice would not like to work. Such a theory was propounded by a researcher called McGregor and this theory was called Theory X.

   Today if you ask officials, they are very optimistic of the people in an organisation as employees and believe that if they are given the right opportunities and are adequately trained, then people as employees love to work and enjoy the challenges that work provides.

   The approach that assumes that people are not inherently lazy is called Theory Y, and it assumes that people have a psychological need to be recognised and enjoy a high self esteem by seeking to achieve good performances and so, enjoy a higher social status in society. The Theory Y perspective prevails within the field of Organisational Behaviour today.

3. **OB recognises the dynamic nature of organisations:** OB scientists recognise that organisations are not static, but dynamic and ever changing. They recognise that organisations are open systems, i.e. self sustaining systems that are constantly in the process of processing input into output.

   For example, as a human resources function, organisations take skilled manpower from society, train them and make them capable of creating products and services that the organisation specialises in. These are further sold back in the society and community. When people buy these products or services, in turn organisational employees make more and the cycle continues.

4. **OB assumes that there is no one best approach:** What is the best leadership style to be adopted? What motivates people to bring out the best in them? Should important decisions be made by groups or individuals? There is no one best answer for all these points.

   This means that OB uses a Contingency Approach. An orientation that recognises that behaviour in work settings is the complex result of many interacting factors.

1.2 DISCIPLINES CONTRIBUTING TO ORGANISATIONAL BEHAVIOUR

Organisational Behaviour is built on the contributions from a number of behavioural sciences such as Psychology, Sociology, Anthropology and Political Science.

1. **Psychology:** Psychology is the scientific study of human and animal behaviour with the object of understanding why living beings behave in a certain way. It deals with the study of individual behaviour and its reasons. It includes topics like learning, perception, personality, training, leadership effectiveness, needs and motivational forces etc.

2. **Social Psychology:** It is the study of relations between people and groups. It has made significant contributions in the areas of measuring, understanding and changing attitudes, communication patterns etc.

3. **Sociology:** It is the study of society. It is a social science that studies how humans behave in a society. It has contributed to OB through the study of group dynamics, work groups, organisational cultures, organisational theory and structure, power, conflicts and intergroup behaviour.

4. **Anthropology:** It is the study of different societies. It helps in gaining understanding of organisational culture, organisational environments and differences between cultures.

5. **Political Science:** It is the social science that deals with the study of behaviour of individuals and groups within a political environment. It predicts the behaviour of people in organisations by looking at it through a political perspective.

1.3 EMERGING TRENDS IN ORGANISATIONAL BEHAVIOUR

Organisations have witnessed a great development from the olden times particularly in respect of structure, operations and people. There is a considerable change in the cross-culture environment, influence of MNCs, growth in the technical know-how and quality management which has provided different environment in the modern organisations. Some of the important trends observed are mentioned below:

1. **Globalisation:** Organisations in recent days have changed the style of working and tried to spread worldwide.

Trapping new market place, new technology or reducing cost through specialisation or cheap labour are a few of the different reasons that motivates organisations to become global. Moreover the way companies integrate their business practices with other countries has also changed. Instead of controlling the whole supply chain, countries outsource some part of it to gain advantage of specialisation. Thomas Friedman highlights this phenomenon in his book "The world is flat" There are several types of organisational changes that has occurred to help business adopt to globalisation, as the old principles no longer work in the age of globalisation. Strategic changes, technological change, change in organisational culture including organisational structural change and a redesign of work tasks are some of the important one. In line with these changes, there is a strong expectation of employees to improve their knowledge and become an integral part of successful business formula in order to respond to the challenges brought by the global economy. In other words it leads to formation of a learning organisation, which is characterised by creating, gaining and transferring the knowledge, and thus constantly modifying the organisational behaviour.

2.   Emerging Employment Relationship: Changing trends in organisations in recent years have made it utmost important to consider some of the emerging employee relations issues which can affect employers in the coming decades. Understanding these issues will help management to plan better and respond to changes in the workplace. Employer employee relationship is also showing change in the modern era. Employers are no more autocrats and participative style of leadership is welcomed. Flexible working hours and increased authority motivates employees to perform their best. Management now welcomes upward communication and participation of lower level employees in the decision making process.

3.   Changing Workforce: The demography of the workforce has changed in the recent years. This is due to a number of factors such as an aging population, labour shortages and immigration. Another significant factor that has changed the workforce is the changes in the attitude of workers. Employers need to adapt their recruitment, training and management processes to adapt to changing workforce. An example of this is that where employers may have previously looked to younger people as a source of recruits, they may now have to broaden their view as there are currently a large number of older people either currently employed or seeking employment. These people may need extra training to bring their skills upto date.

New parents now want to work closer to home or work from home, employers may find that they need to make this a possible option in order to retain old employees or find new staff. Allowing people to work from home will also make the employer and job more attractive to a wider range of people.

Nowadays organisations are also witnessing a shortage of skilled labour in many sectors. Hence employers may have to take on less skilled workers initially and develop them, rather than simply hiring experienced people. Hiring employees from overseas also serves the purpose.

4.   Knowledge Management: Knowledge management is a structured activity that improves an organisation's capacity to acquire, share, and utilise knowledge for its survival and success. Knowledge management is around us from a very long period of time in one or the other form. The decisions we make and the action we take both are enabled by knowledge of some type. Hence to improve quality of these actions and decisions is important to understand the process of knowledge management.

Studies in knowledge management have proved an inseparable relationship between knowledge management and organisational culture. Research has also proved that organisational culture is a major barrier to leveraging intellectual assets. They focus on four ways in which culture influences organisational behaviours which is central to knowledge creation, sharing, and use. The first is the shared assumptions about what knowledge is and which knowledge is worth managing. Second is the relationship between individual and organisational knowledge. Third is the context for social interaction that determines how knowledge will be used in particular situations. Fourth is the process by which knowledge is created, legitimated, and distributed in organisations.

There are three basic elements of knowledge management.

(i) Knowledge Acquisition: It is a method of learning through experiences, sensation or perception.

(ii) Knowledge Sharing: Knowledge sharing is a process through which knowledge is shared among family, friends or any community.

(iii) Knowledge Dissemination: It is conceptual and instrumental use of new knowledge. Increased awareness and ability to make informed choice among available alternatives are the outcomes of knowledge dissemination.

Knowledge Maps: Knowledge maps guide employees to understand what knowledge is needed to increase their efficiency and productivity and where this knowledge is located.

5. Information Technology and OB: Technological change and advancement is one of the most salient factors impacting organisations and employees today. In particular, the prominence of Information Technology (IT) has grown many folds in recent years. This innovation in IT has opened new ways for conducting business that are different from the past. Technology has changed the nature of work as well as the roles of employees. Managerial decision making, stress handling, and attitude towards work have changed as an impact of technology. It is also seen from decades that there is a normal tendency of human being to resist changes, making adoption of new technologies a little difficult. It has become important for the business and management to understand and take these issues into consideration while introducing or implementing new technology. Frequent sessions on change management can help employees understand, use and adopt new technologies easily.

1.4 CHALLENGES AND OPPORTUNITIES FOR ORGANISATIONAL BEHAVIOUR

OB offers a number of challenges and opportunities for managers. It can help in improving the quality and productivity of organisations. This can be done by ways listed below:

1. By giving its employees opportunities to participate in planning and bringing about changes within the organisations.

2. OB through its vast study areas helps a manager to improve people skills by being a good listener and giving proper feedback.

3. OB recognises the fact that two persons are not the same. Work force diversity, if managed properly, can increase creativity and improve decision-making by bringing about diverse perspectives into view.

4. It provides guidelines for understanding differences between national cultures which may also result in change in management practices.

OB has lead to putting more confidence in the employees. Managers learn how to give up control and employees learn how to take responsibility of their work and take correct decisions. Thus empowerment is an outcome of OB. It is a challenge for managers to enhance employee creativity and acceptability for change so that organisations can maintain flexibility and remain successful.

1.5 ORGANISATIONAL BEHAVIOUR ACROSS CULTURE

1. Conditions affecting Multinational Operations: Today many organisations do business in more than one country. These multinational organisations add new dimensions to organisational behaviour as communication lines are lengthened and control often becomes difficult. In this context, it is necessary that managers acquire both language and intercultural skills in dealing with people – customers, suppliers, competitors and colleagues from other countries as they are taking a risky step into different social, legal, political and economic environments- the primary conditions affecting multinational operations.

(i) Social Condition: The overriding social conditions affecting multinational operations are:

(a) Poorly developed human resources which limit the ability to employ local labour productively.

(b) Needed skills are temporarily imported from other countries and vast training programmes begin to prepare local workers.

(c) Local culture not being familiar with advanced technology or complex organisation.

(d) Differences in work ethic of employees across cultures.

(i) Legal and Ethical Conditions: The overriding Legal and Ethical conditions affecting multinational operations are:

(a) Differences across countries in their legal systems and especially in their relevant employment laws and business practices.

(b) Differences across countries in the judicial system regarding time for disposition of cases and penalties for seemingly minor offences.

(c) Differences across countries in local mores, customs and ethical behaviours.

(d) The treatment of women and other minorities to prohibit workplace discrimination.

(ii) Political Conditions: The overriding Political conditions affecting multinational operations are:

(a) Instability of the government of the host country spills over onto organisations that wish to establish or expand operations in the host country, making them cautious of further investments. This organisational instability leaves workers insecure and causes them to be passive and low in initiative.

(b) Strong nationalistic drive may impel locals to desire to run their country and their organisations by themselves, without interference by foreign nationals- a foreign manager simply may not be welcome.

(c) Organized labour in many nations is not an independent force but is mostly an arm of the authoritarian state. In other nations labour is somewhat independent, but it is socialistic, class-conscious and oriented towards political action more than direct negotiation with organisations. Employers find that the state tends to be involved in collective bargaining and other practices like employee layoffs and employee transfers affecting workers.

(ii) Economic Conditions: The overriding Economic conditions affecting multinational operations are:

(a) Low per capita income.

(b) Rapid inflation making the economic life of workers insecure. It encourages them to spend rapidly, not to save for retirement security, develops their dependence on the government which is often incapable of responding and gives rise to social unrest.

2. Managing an International Workforce: Whenever the geographical boundaries of an organisation spans over two or more countries, it will then face the challenge of blending various cultures. Multiculturalism occurs when the employees in two or more cultures interact with each other on a regular basis. Expatriates (both parent country nationals from the nation in which home office is located or third country nationals from some other nations) need to adjust their leadership styles, communication patterns and other practices to fit the culture of their host country

An expatriate manager may find several obstacles to a smooth adaptation to a new culture. An early requirement for overcoming such obstacles is to acquire cultural awareness of the multiple ways in which cultures differ.

3. Individual Differences: Five major dimensions that result in sharpest differences among employees include:

(i) Individualism/Collectivism: Cultures that emphasize individualism tend to accent individual rights and freedoms, have very closely knit social networks and place considerable attention on self respect. Collectivism heavily accents the group and values harmony among members. Individual feelings are subordinated to the group's overall good. Face saving (maintaining one's self image in front of others) is highly important in collectivistic cultures.

(ii) Power Distance: Power distance refers to the belief that strong and legitimate decision making rights separate managers and employees in different cultures.

(iii) Uncertainty Avoidance: Uncertainty avoidance is the value for clarity and preference to avoid ambiguity at work in different cultures.

(iv) Masculinity and Femininity: Masculinity and femininity is the way of defining gender roles in more traditional and stereotypical ways or having a broader viewpoint on the great variety of roles that both males and females can play at the workplace and at home in different cultures.

(v) Time Orientation: Time orientation is the accent cultures place on necessity of preparing for future or valuing the past and emphasizing on present.

Individual differences also occur due to the differences in culture on the emphasis it places on using situational cues to develop a complete portrait of a visitor. High context cultures tend to emphasise personal relations, place high value on trust, focus on nonverbal cues and accent the need to attend to social needs before business matters. Low context cultures tend to rely on written rules and legal documents, conduct business first and value expertise and performance.

1.6 MODELS AND APPROACHES OF ORGANISATIONAL BEHAVIOUR

There are different models of OB. Some of them are in practice while others have become outdated. Within an organisation, there may be more than one model being practiced by different departments. Different managers may adopt different models according to their personal preferences.

1.6.1 OB Models

The various OB Models are discussed below in detail:

1. **The Autocratic Model:** This model lays emphasis on power. It believes that the persons in commanding position must have the power to demand from their subordinates and an employee who does not follow orders will be penalised. The autocratic management believes that in order to get the desired output; employees must be directed, persuaded and pushed into performance. Thus the management's approach is authoritative, formal and official. Employees are submissive to their managers, but out of apprehension rather than respect. This affects employees' morale adversely as they are over-dependent on their managers and have a feeling of discontent and insecurity towards management.

2. **The Custodial Model:** This model lays emphasis on money rather than power and leads to employees' over-dependence on an organisation. The custodial management tries to satisfy the security needs of employees and use it as a motivating force. It provides its employees with several economic rewards and benefits which keep them well maintained and satisfied. However organisations not having sufficient wealth to provide pensions and other benefits, cannot follow a custodial approach. The disadvantage of this approach is that it makes the employees over-contented and results in poor performance and low levels of motivation and cooperation.

3. **The Supportive Model:** Unlike the previous two models, this model lays emphasis on leadership rather than power or money. Supportive management tries to create an environment that encourages employees to grow and accomplish what they are capable of. Management's approach is to support the employee's job performance rather than to simply support employee benefit payments. It believes that workers are not passive or resistant to work by nature and they will come forward to take responsibility and contribute, if management provides them a chance.

   This model brings in a feeling of belongingness and participation among the employees towards the organisation. Thus this model is beneficial as compared to autocratic and custodial models since employees are more strongly motivated as their status and recognition needs are met in a better manner.

4. **The Collegial Model:** The term "collegial" refers to people working together as a group. This model is an extension of the supportive mode and lays emphasis on creating a sense of partnership with employees. Managers are seen as joint contributors rather than as bosses.

   The management's approach is supporting teamwork and being the employees' coach. As a result employees get the sense of self-discipline, responsibility and obligation to uphold quality standards that will bring credit to their jobs and company. Another advantage of this approach is that in this kind of environment employees normally feel some degree of fulfilment, worthwhile contribution, and self-actualisation, even though the employee benefits may be modest. Employees feel that managers are also contributing towards their success, they are easily accepted and respected by them.

5. **The System Model:** This model lays emphasis on building a relationship with employees based on trust. Management's approach is to demonstrate a sense of care and being sensitive to the needs of a diverse workforce with rapidly changing needs and complex personal and family needs. As a result employees get self–motivated and perform better as they are committed to organisational goals. Thus employees develop a feeling of ownership for the organisation and its product and services.

1.6.2 Approaches to OB

Organisational framework is based on various approaches as discussed below:
1. Classical
2. Human Relations including neo-human relations
3. Systems
4. Contingency
5. Decision Making
6. Social Action
7. Postmodernism

1. **Classical Approach:** This approach considers an organisation in terms of its purpose and formal structure. It lay emphasis on planning of work, technical requirements of

the organisation, principles of management and assumptions of rational and logical behaviour. Analysis of organisation is associated with work and has been written by Taylor, Urwick, Mooney, and Reiley.

Classical writers are also known as formal and scientific management writers. All of them were concerned with improving the organisational structure by means of increasing efficiency.

Mooney and **Reiley** set out a number of common principles which relate to all types of organisations. They place particular attention on:

- The principle of co-ordination – the need for people to act together with unity of action, the exercise of authority and the need for discipline.
- The scalar principle – the hierarchy of organisation, the grading of duties and the process of delegation.
- The functional principle – specialisation and the distinction between different kinds of duties.

2. **Human Relations including Neo-Human Relations Approach:** The main emphasis of the classical writers was on structure and the formal organisation, but during the 1920s, i.e. the years of the Great Depression, greater attention began to be paid to the social factors at work and to the behaviour of employees within an organisation – that is, to human relations.

These experiments have been criticised a lot especially the Hawthorne experiment. The criticism was against the human relations approach and it was believed that it is insufficiently scientific and too narrow. It ignores the role of the organisation itself and how society operates.

There were four main phases to the Hawthorne experiments:

- The illumination experiments
- The relay assembly test room
- The interviewing programme
- The bank wiring observation room.

Neo-Human Relations: To overcome the limitations of the human relations approach, the writers in the 1950s and 1960s adopted a more psychological orientation. New ideas on management theory arose and a major focus was on the personal adjustment of an individual within the work organisation and the effects of group relationships and leadership styles. This group of writers is often categorised separately under the heading of 'neo-human relations'.

Famous contributors to the neo-classical approach are **Herzberg** and **McGregor**. Herzberg perceived two sets of factors affecting motivation and satisfaction at work. He also mentioned the 'hygiene or maintenance factors' which are concerned with the basic job related environment.

The neo-human relations approach has generated a large amount of writing and research, not only from the original profounder, but also from others seeking to establish the validity of their ideas. This has led to continuing attention being given to such matters as organisation structuring, group dynamics, job satisfaction, communication and participation, leadership styles and motivation.

3. **The Systems Approach:** The systems approach attempts to reconcile these two earlier approaches and the work of the formal and the informal writers. Attention is focused on the total work organisation and the interrelationships of structure and behaviour and the range of variables within the organisation. This approach can be contrasted with a view of the organisation as separate parts. The systems approach encourages managers to view the organisation both as a whole and as part of a larger environment. The idea is that any part of an organisation's activities affects all other parts.

4. **The Contingency Approach:** This shows concern with the importance of structure and places emphasis on general sets of principles while the human relations approach gave little attention to structure. In contrast, the contingency approach emphasised the importance of structure as it has a significant influence on organisational performance.

   The contingency approach, which can be seen as an extension of the systems approach, highlights possible means of differentiating among alternative forms of organisational structures and systems of management. It believes that there is no single optimum state. For example, the structure of the organisation and it's 'success' are dependent upon the nature of tasks with which it is designed to deal and the nature of environmental influences.

   The most appropriate structure and system of management is therefore dependent upon the contingencies of the situation for each particular organisation. The contingency approach implies that organisation's theory should not seek to suggest one best way to structure or manage organisations but should provide insights into the situational and contextual factors which influence management decisions.

5. **The Decision-Making Approach:** The systems approach involves the functions which are directly concerned with the achievement of objectives and the identification of main decision areas or sub-systems. Viewing the organisation as a system emphasises the need for good information and channels of communication in order to assist effective decision-making in the organisation. Recognition of the need for decision-making and the attainment of goals draw attention to a sub-division of the systems approach, or a separate category, that of the decision-making (decision theory) approach. Here the focus is on managerial decision-making and how organisations process and use information in making decisions.

   Leading writers on the decision-making approach include **Barnard**, **Simon** and **Cyert** and **March**. The scope of the decision-making approach, however, is wide and it is possible to identify contributions from engineers, mathematicians and operational research specialists in addition to the work of economists, psychologists and writers on management and organisation.

Barnard focused on the needs for co-operative action in organisations. He believed that people's ability to communicate and their commitment and contribution to the achievement of a common purpose were necessary for the existence of a co-operative system. These ideas were developed further by Simon. He sees management as a means to decision-making and his concern is with how decisions are made and how decision-making can be improved.

Simon criticises the implication of man as completely rational and proposes a model of an 'administrative man' who, unlike an 'economic man', 'satisfies' rather than 'maximises'. Administrative decision-making is the achievement of satisfactory rather than optimal results in solving problems.

6. **Social Action Approach:** Social action represents a contribution from sociologists to the study of organisations. Social action writers attempt to view the organisation from the perspective of individual members (actors), who will each have their own goals and interpretation of their work situation in terms of the satisfaction sought and the meaning of work for them. The goals of the individual, and the means selected and actions taken to achieve these goals are affected by the individual's perception of the situation. Social action looks to the individual's own definition of the situation as a basis for explaining behaviour. Conflict of interests is seen as normal behaviour and part of organisational life.

7. **Postmodernism:** The work of contemporary writers discussed above together with the achievements of practitioners such as Alfred P. Sloan Jr (1875–1966, Chief Executive and Honorary Chairman of General Motors), gave rise to the so-called 'modern organisation'. With the development of the information and technological age, a more recent view of organisations and management is the idea of postmodernism. In the 1990s, writers such as **Clegg** described the postmodern organisation in terms of the influence of technological determinism, structural flexibility, premised on niches, multi-skilled jobs marked by a lack of demarcation and more complex employment relationships including subcontracting and networking.

1.7 IMPORTANCE OF ORGANISATIONAL BEHAVIOUR

- **Controlling and Directing Behaviour:** After understanding the mechanism of human behaviour, managers are required to control and direct the behaviour so that it conforms to the standards required for achieving the organisational objectives. Thus, managers are required to control and direct the behaviour at all levels of individual interaction. Therefore, organisational behaviour helps managers in controlling and directing in different areas such as use of power and sanction, leadership, communication and building organisational climate favourable for better interaction.

- **Use of Power and Sanction:** The behaviours can be controlled and directed by the use of power and sanction, which are formally defined by the organisation. Power is referred to as the capacity of an individual to take certain action and may be utilised in many ways. Organisational behaviour explains how various means of power and sanction can be utilised so that both organisational and individual objectives are achieved simultaneously.

- **Leadership:** Organisational behaviour brings new insights and understanding to the practice and theory of leadership. It identifies various leadership styles available to a manager and analyses which style is more appropriate in a given situation. Thus, managers can adopt styles keeping in view the various dimensions of organisations, individuals and situations.

- **Communication:** Communication helps people to come in contact with each other. To achieve organisational objectives, the communication must be effective. The communication process and its work in inter-personal dynamics have been evaluated by organisational behaviour.

- **Organisational Climate:** Organisational climate refers to the total organisational situations affecting human behaviour. Organisational climate takes a system perspective that affect human behaviour. Besides improving the satisfactory working conditions and adequate compensation, organisational climate includes creation of an atmosphere of effective supervision; the opportunity for the realisation of personal goals, congenial relations with others at the work place and a sense of accomplishment.

- **Organisational Adaptation:** Organisations, as dynamic entities are characterised by pervasive changes. Organisations have to adapt themselves to the environmental changes by making suitable, internal arrangements such as convincing employees who normally have the tendency of resisting any changes.

1.7.1 Limitations of Organisational Behaviour

Some of the limitations of Organisational Behaviour are:

- Organisational behaviour cannot abolish conflict and frustration but can reduce them. It is a way to improve but not an absolute answer to problems.

- It is only one of the many systems operating within a large social system.

- People who lack system understanding may develop a 'behavioural basis', which gives them a narrow view point, i.e., a tunnel vision that emphasises on satisfying employee experiences while overlooking the broader system of an organisation in relation to all its public.

- The law of diminishing returns also operates in the case of organisational behaviour. It states, that at some point increase of a desirable practice starts to produce declining returns and sometimes, negative returns.

- The concept implies that for any situation there is an optimum amount of a desirable practice. When that point is exceeded, there is a decline in returns. For example, too much security may lead to less employee initiative and growth. This relationship shows that organisational effectiveness is achieved not by maximising one human variable but by working all system variables together in a balanced way.

- A significant concern about organisational behaviour is that its knowledge and techniques could be used to manipulate people without regard for human welfare. People who lack ethical values could use people in unethical ways.

Although organisational behaviour does have limitations, these limitations should not blind us to the tremendous potential that O. B. can contribute to the advancement of civilisation. It has provided and will provide much improvement in the human environment.

By building a better climate for people, organisational behaviour will release their creative potential to help solve major social problems. In this way organisational behaviour may contribute to social improvements that stretch far beyond the confines of any one organisation. A better climate may help some person a major breakthrough in solar energy, health, or education.

Improved organisational behaviour is not easy to apply. But the opportunities are there. It should produce a higher quality of life in which there is improved harmony within each person, among people, and among the organisations of the future.

1.8 ORGANISATIONAL CHANGE

The real world is turbulent, requiring organisations and their members to undergo dynamic change if they are to perform at competitive levels.

If environments were perfectly static, if employees' skills and abilities were always up to date and incapable of deteriorating, and if tomorrows were exactly same as today, organisation change would have little or no importance for managers.

Managers are the primary change agents in most organisations and they shape the organisation's change culture through the decisions they make and by their role-modeling behaviour.

Management decisions related to structural designs, cultural factors, and human resource policies largely determine the level of innovation within the organisation. Management decisions, policies and practices will determine the degree to which the organisation learns and adapts to changing environmental factors.

1.8.1 Meaning of Organisational Change

In the modern business environment, organisations face rapid changes like never before. Globalisation and the constant innovation of technology result in a constantly evolving business environment. Phenomena such as social media and mobile adaptability have revolutionised business and the effect of this, is an ever increasing, need for change and therefore change management.

Organisation change occurs when business strategies or major sections of an organisation are altered. Also, known as, reorganisation, restructuring and turnaround. Organisational change is a structured approach in an organisation for ensuring that changes are smoothly and successfully implemented to achieve lasting benefits.

Due to globalisation, the modern business environment is changing rapidly and so is the technology. Organisations have to face these changes constantly. Emergence of various new trends such as social media and mobile applications has brought in revolutionary changes in the way businesses operate today. Organisations are also said to have changed when they change their business strategies or major divisions. These are termed as reorganisation, restructuring and turnaround.

All this has resulted into the need for change management for most of the organisations. Organisational change is a structured approach undertaken to ensure that changes are introduced smoothly and implemented successfully to survive in the evolving business environment and gain a competitive advantage over others.

Organisations must be able to deal with the changes comfortably and hence the ability of managers to manage and adapt to organisational change has become crucial today.

Organisational change affects all the departments and all the levels in an organisation directly. Thus the entire company must learn how to handle changes in the organisation.

1.8.2 Nature of Organisational Change

We know that change offers both life to the organisation and also threatens the existence of life. Those who fail to obey demand of time have to face adverse consequences. Some people, though willing, find it difficult to adopt certain types of changes because of lack of capabilities. Nature of change can be better discussed with reference to following features:

1. Change is an essential phenomenon, and, hence, it is inevitable (unavoidable). People have to change to take advantage of change.
2. Change demands alteration in the established way of life. It forces people to adjust and readjust with new things, foregoing the existing ones.
3. Change brings opportunities or troubles (threats), depending upon the capacity of people, and how it is managed.
4. It is a base for growth and development because it offers plenty of opportunities for development.
5. Organisation responds to its environment by inviting and implementing change. Therefore, it is a form of organisation's response to its environment. Similarly, change is also implemented because of internal needs or forces,
6. Change may be economic or non-economic, direct or indirect, immediate or gradual, partial or total, and so on.
7. Resistance to change is a common problem faced by most organisations. People resist the change due to a number of reasons.

8. Successful implementation (if change requires planned intervention (systematic plan) based on study and analysis of a number of considerations.

9. Most managers work as a catalyst whose task is to absorb change in the very interest of the organisation. Sometimes, external professional consultants also perform the same task.

10. Change is always in form of addition, replacement, improvement or subtraction of something.

1.8.3 Levels of Change

Change can be at individual, group and organisational level.

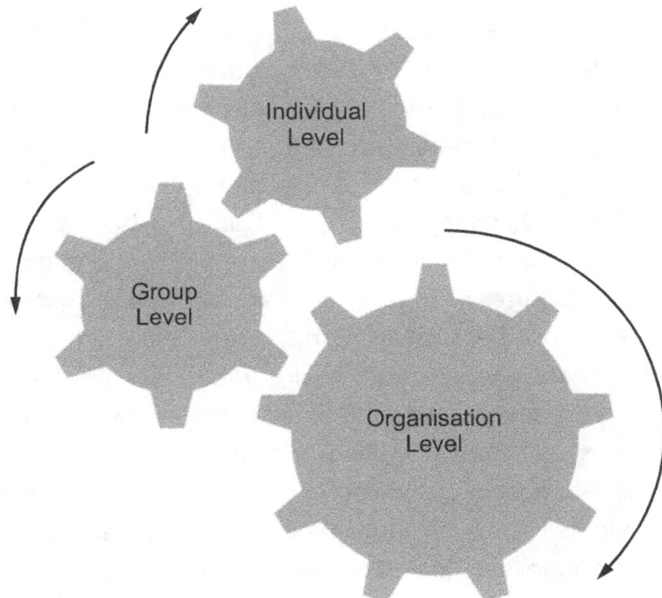

Fig. 1.1: Levels of Change

1. **Individual Level Change:** At the individual level, change is reflected in developments such as changes in a job assignment, physical move to a different location or the changes in maturity of a person which occurs over time. Changes at the individual level will have significant implication for the total organisation. A manager, who desires to implement a major change at the individual level, transferring an employee for instance, must understand that the change will have repercussions beyond the individual.

2. **Group Level Change:** Most organisations implement change at the group level. It is because of group activity. The group could be departments or informal work groups. Changes at the group level can affect work, efficiency and behaviour at the work and social organisation and status system.

Managers should take groups into consideration while bringing change into the system however informal groups can pose a major barrier because they have majority of strength. Formal groups can resist change by the way of unions.

3. **Organisational Change:** Changes at this level involve major programmes that affect both individuals and groups. Such decisions are made at the top level. It requires longer duration and detailed planning to implement this change.

1.8.4 Types of Change

(A) Changes Related to People

1. **Personnel Change:** Sometimes changes are a direct result of other organisational changes. Or else, companies simply seek to change worker's attitudes and behaviours in order to increase their effectiveness. **Bateman** and **Zeithaml** suggest that attempting a strategic change, introducing a new technology and other changes in the work environment may affect people's attitudes (sometimes in a negative way). Frequently, management initiates programmes with a conscious goal of directly and positively changing the people themselves. The science of organisational development deals with changing people. This may be done on the job through techniques such as education and training, team building and career planning.

2. **Culture Change:** Culture change within an organisation aims at changing the behaviour patterns of the organisation's employees. Some examples of culture change include reward-and-recognition programmes, employee empowerment and training. These programmes attempt to improve motivation and decision-making skills and to increase sensitivity to diversity issues.

3. **People-centred Change:** People-centred process changes attempt to alter the attitudes, behaviours, skills or performance of employees within an organisation. Communication, employee motivation, leadership and group interaction are some primary focuses of people-centred change. This type of change may affect the employees and their behaviours in many areas. Some examples are: improved problem-solving skills, the way employees learn new skills, and how employees perceive themselves, their jobs and the organisation.

4. **Social Change:** Social change refers to the modification of established relationships in the organisation. Social change encompasses the large set of goals that organisations establish around people. This includes an empowered workforce, collaborative work arrangements and matching personal fulfilment to organisational needs.

(B) Changes Related to Organisations

1. **Leadership Change:** Leadership transitions are critical. Transitions in leadership offer an opportunity to make changes in many areas of the organisation. The situation is fluid or, in Lewin's framework of organisational change, 'unfrozen.' "The transition is

an occasion to rethink the commitment to the present agenda, to reflect on roads not taken in the past and to review future choices. Many significant changes – in policy, people, organisational structure and procedures – are more easily introduced simultaneously with a leadership change.

2. **Structural Change:** Changes within an organisation's structure can occur due to external influences. Structural changes may involve structural characteristics, administrative procedures or management systems. They may involve simple policy changes or be as complex as a complete restructuring of the management hierarchy.

3. **Reengineering:** Change centred on reengineering focuses on making major structural changes in the organisation. Implementation of these changes typically focus on everyday tasks or procedures. The goal is to substantially improve productivity, efficiency, quality and customer satisfaction.

4. **Incremental Organisational Change:** Incremental change is a step-by-step approach to re-designing an organisation. Each small increment that is changed produces changes in other parts of the organisation. By changing specific processes or portions, the entire organisation changes over time.

5. **Fundamental Organisational Change:** When major organisational changes are necessary and time constraints are a significant factor, a more radical transformation becomes essential. Fundamental organisational change focuses on changing major characteristics of the entire organisation rather than specific parts.

6. **Paradigm Shift:** Sometimes the basic rules of the game shift and such shift is not predetermined. Some people and companies simply start to work with it and begin to achieve new levels of success. This phenomenon is known as a "paradigm shift." Many people use the term loosely - but very few actually understand it until it becomes the brick wall that stands in the way of progress.

7. **Strategic Change:** Strategic changes involve long-term planning while incorporating a strong external orientation. These changes may cover major functional areas of an organisation. This type of change may occur while adjusting the firm's strategy to achieve the goals of the company. This type of change may also result in a change to the mission statement of the organisation. An organisation's approach to doing business, targeted markets, partnerships or the types of products sold may be included in the strategic change approach.

(C) Changes Related to Systems

1. **Process-oriented Change:** The goal of process-oriented change is to improve productivity. Process-oriented change affects the way in which an organisation delivers services, produces products and handles current business practices. As the environmental factors of an organisation change, the need for process-oriented change increases.

2. **Technological Change:** This type of approach concerns the implementation or integration of technology into the processes of an organisation. Primarily, technology includes large hardware or software systems.

3. **Systems Change:** Systems change means making a change that endures and changes the heart of the organisation. Such change is systematic and needs time, planning and patience. It is not done by just tweaking parts of the system in isolation. But, it means ultimately impacting change across all elements of the system.

4. **Continuous Improvement:** Continuous improvement entails finding the best practices, adapting them and continually improving them. When using these ideas to encourage constant improvement; new product and service ideas, new processes, and opportunities for growth become the norm.

   The process of continuous improvement occurs by developing a series of measureable processes. The next step is to acknowledge and correct defects.

5. **Continual Change:** Continual change is similar to continuous process improvement but is a broader term. This builds on the philosophy that when change stops, companies cease to exist. Continual change to optimise technological breakthroughs is required for an organisation to systemically evolve. This change continues until it has exhausted the improvement that is known.

6. **Transactional Change:** Transactional change occurs in a situation in which the organisation experiences some feature of change but the fundamental nature of the organisation remains the same. This may include a company's organisational climate, which encompasses the perceptions and attitudes of people about the organisation. Transactional change includes changes to structure, management practices and systems.

7. **Business Process Reengineering:** Business process reengineering is the redesign of business processes and the associated systems and organisational structures. The goal of this type of change is to achieve a dramatic improvement in business performance.

(D) Change in General

1. **Growth:** Growth needs to be managed on multiple levels i.e. the right leaders, leading the right people, to do the right things, at the right time.

2. **Unplanned Change:** Unplanned change usually occurs because of a major and sudden surprise to the organisation. This causes its members to respond in a highly reactive and disorganised fashion.

   At times, organisational change happens when it becomes necessary to react to a sudden development. Emergency can force organisations to introduce new ways of doing things or to restructure themselves.

3. **Planned Change:** Planned change occurs when leaders in the organisation recognise the need for a major change and proactively organise a plan to accomplish the change. Planned change occurs with successful implementation of a strategic plan, reorganisation plan or other types of plan for implementation of a change of this magnitude.

4. **Radical Change:** Radical change is a process by which firms regain competitive advantage after it has been lost or threatened significantly. The type and extent of change undertaken depends upon the firm's resources and capabilities, its competitive environment and its leadership. Radical change is divergent and meant to fundamentally change the firm's processes, systems, structures, strategies and core values.

5. **Developmental Change:** Developmental change concentrates on improving an already successful environment. Development occurs through improving aspects of an organisation such as increasing customer base or introducing a product expansion.

6. **Transformational Change:** Transformational change occurs when organisations implement drastic changes and essentially transform themselves. This can occur when an organisation faces different technologies, significant changes in supply and demand, unexpected competition, lack of revenue or other major shifts in the way they do business.

    Transformational change is where the organisation is fundamentally and substantially altered. Organisational culture is part of transformational change and is harder to change as against organisational climate because of its deeply-rooted beliefs and values. Included in transformational change are mission and strategy, leadership and organisational culture.

7. **Transitional Change:** Transitional change involves the replacement of a current process with a process that is new to the company. Mergers, acquisitions, new product creation and the implementation of new technologies are examples of transitional change.

    Transitional change requires the introduction of new processes that modify the way the company operates, in the event that current methods of operation are no longer applicable. Examples of transitional change include reorganisation, minor restructuring, utilisation of new operational techniques / methods / procedures or the introduction of new services or products.

8. **Strategy Deployment:** These projects are defined as building or changing the capabilities of the organisation. Some efforts involve trying to improve what the organisation does and other efforts involve creating radically new strengths.

9. **Restructuring / Downsizing:** These projects involve rearranging organisational units and / or the workforce. Downsizing primarily refers to reducing the number of employees and it also includes divestiture of company assets, that is, selling off a piece of the business. It is based upon quantitative measure of operational and financial performance.

10. **Remedial Change:** Remedial change addresses a particular situation, which needs immediate attention. For example, a deficiency in a product line or employee burnout. It is said to be successful when there is a solution to the problem.

11. **Evolutionary Change:** Evolutionary change involves setting direction, allocating responsibilities and establishing reasonable timelines for achieving objectives. However it is not fast enough or comprehensive enough to move ahead of the curve, in an evolving world, where stakes are high and the response time is short.

12. **Revolutionary Change:** When faced with market-driven urgency, abrupt and sometimes disruptive changes happen. Dramatic downsizing or reengineering may be required to keep the company competitive. In situations where time is critical to success and companies must become more efficient and productive rapidly, revolutionary change is demanded.

13. **Proactive Change:** Proactive change involves actively attempting to make alterations to the work place and its practices. Companies that take a proactive approach to change often try to avoid a potential future threat or to capitalise on a potential future opportunity.

14. **Reactive Change:** Reactive change occurs when an organisation makes changes in its practices after the occurrence of some threat or opportunity.

Forces for Change

1. **Organisations face a dynamic and changing environment:** This requires adaptation. Six specific forces that are acting as stimulants for change are limited focus to change, threat to expertise, group inertia, structural inertia, threat to established power relationships and threat to established resource allocation.

2. **The changing nature of the workforce:**
    - A multicultural environment.
    - Human resource policies and practices changed to attract and keep this more diverse workforce.
    - Large expenditure on training to upgrade reading, maths, computer, and other skills of employees

3. **Technology is changing jobs and organisations:**
    - Sophisticated information technology is also making organisations more responsive. As organisations have had to become more adaptable, so too have their employees.
    - We live in an "age of discontinuity." Beginning in the early 1970s with the overnight quadrupling of world oil prices, economic shocks have continued to impose changes on organisations.

4. **Competition is changing:**
    - The global economy means global competitors.
    - Established organisations need to defend themselves against both traditional competitors and small, entrepreneurial firms with innovative offerings.
    - Successful organisations will be the ones that can change in response to the competition.

5. **Social trends during the past generation suggest changes that organisations have to adjust for:**
    - The expansion of the Internet, Baby Boomers retiring, and people moving from the suburbs back to cities.
    - A global context for OB is required. No one could have imagined how world politics would change in recent years.
    - September 11th has caused changes organisations have made in terms of practices concerning security, back-up systems, employee stereotyping, etc.

1.8.5 Resistance to Change

Resistance to change is understood to be a natural phenomenon. But not all changes are resisted. In many organisations changes are accepted instead of being resisted. People have a natural instinct to accept change. Sources of resistance to change may be **rational or emotional.** Rational resistance occurs when people do not have proper information about the change.

Emotional resistance is the feeling of resistance to change evoked due to the people's perception of how the change will affect them.

Resistance to change is normal and people cling to habits and to the status quo. Managerial actions can minimise or arouse resistance. People must be motivated to get away from old habits. This must take place in stages rather than abruptly so that "managed change" takes on the character of "natural change." In addition to normal inertia, organisation change introduces anxieties about the future. If the future after the change is perceived positively, resistance will be less.

Education and communication are therefore key ingredients in minimising negative reactions.

Employees can be informed about both the nature of the change and the logic behind it before it takes place through reports, memos, group presentations or individual discussions. Another important component of overcoming resistance is inviting employee participation and involvement, in both the design and implementation phases of the change effort. Organised forms of facilitation and support can be deployed. Managers can ensure that employees will have the resources to bring about the change; they can make themselves available to provide explanations and to minimise stress arising in many situations.

Reasons for Resistance to Change

The basic problem in the management of change is the study of reasons for resistance to change. Change is a persistent phenomenon, but people resist change in the context of their pattern of life or in the context of their situations in the organisation. Change of any type demands readjustment while it is not simple, possible and favourable to all. Hence, resistance to change is also very usual like the change itself.

(A) Economic Causes

1. **Fear of Losing Job or Reduction in Employment:** Due to the change in technology, methods of work, use of automatic machines and quantity or quality of work required; people think that there will be a reduction in their employment opportunities, as they will not be able to cope up with the machines. This fear leads to resistance to change on the part of the workers.

2. **Insecurity of Job:** Generally, change in technology is expected to result in technical unemployment, as old employees may not be able to handle new machines. Hence the fear of unemployment leads to resistance to change. Such resistance is individual as well as collective.

3. **Doubt about Future or Fear of Obsolescence:** Employees may fear that they may be demoted, if they do not possess the new skills required for their jobs, after the introduction of change. There is uncertainty of adjustment, separation of group etc. Hence, they prefer status-quo positions.

4. **Fear and Increased Work Load:** Change in work technology and methods may result in the fear that work-load will be increased, while there will be no corresponding increase in their remuneration. This feeling results in resistance to change.

(B) Personal Causes

1. **Requirement of Training:** If due to changes in technology and work, the organisation requires training and relearning for employees, it may lead to resistance as all persons may not like to undergo refreshers and training courses.

2. **Boredom and Monotony:** If the proposed change is expected to lead to greater specialisation resulting in boredom and monotony, it may also be resisted by people.

3. **Non-involvement in Decision-making:** If employees are not allowed to take part in the decision-making process for change, then they may resist the change. When they do not fully understand the implications of change, they resist it. Some employees resist change as it implies a criticism of the present methods as inadequate or unsuitable for which they may not agree.

(C) Social Causes

1. **Need for New Social Adjustment:** Any organisational change requires new social adjustments with the group, work situation and new employer. All individuals are not ready to accept this challenge. Some people even refuse promotions on this ground as they may have to break their present social contacts.

2. **Taking Change as Pressure of Outside Power:** Some employees take any change as imposed from outside upon them. This happens particularly when change is brought about abruptly. If employees are consulted and given due participation in the process of introducing change; their objection and resistance can be minimised.

3. **Orthodox Mentality:** Some employees consider that every change is for the benefit of the management and enterprise itself, rather than the benefits of employees or even the general public. Hence, they resist change.

Overcoming Resistance to Change

Management is responsible for bringing various changes. Hence, it acts as an agent for the changes. If the management has to introduce change slowly and successfully in the organisation, it has to overcome the resistance and make it a successful venture. An atmosphere for change is to be created. The management must realise that resistance to change is basically a human problem, though on surface, it may appear to be related to technical aspects of change. So, it must be tackled in a human and social manner. In short, the following steps can be taken by management to facilitate change acceptance.

1. **Discussion about the Changes with Workers/Employees:** Before introducing any change, the employees should be fully consulted and they must be made a party to any such decision. The meaning and purpose of the change must be fully communicated to those who will be affected by it. Sufficient time should be allowed for discussion and for inviting their suggestions.

2. **Proper Planning for Change:** Changes should not be forced at once. They should be planned. People should get an opportunity to participate both in planning the change and installing it. This will help the group of the affected people to recognise the need for change and thus prepare themselves for receiving it without any fear. The time, place and quantum of change should be determined and the mode of introduction of change should also be planned.

3. **Protection of the Interest of Employees:** Management should ensure that employees will be protected from economic loss in status or personal dignity. If these things are protected, the degree of resistance to change will be very low.

4. **Group Dynamics:** Group dynamics refers to the everchanging interactions and adjustments in the mutual perceptions and relationships among members of the groups. Such group interactions are the most powerful instruments which facilitate or inhibit adaptation to change. Adaptation is a team activity which requires conformity to the new group norms, criterion, traditions and work patterns and styles. If these could be positively introduced by the management and group-based techniques for introduction of change are adopted, the results are likely to be more successful and durable.

5. **Changes should be Slow in Parts:** The management should not introduce any change at once and abruptly. The management must create awareness of change and develop an ability to be introduced in parts. If possible, the results must be reviewed and if required, adjustments must be made in it. This will not overload the

management with responsibility and the whole system of change can be introduced with tested results at each stage.

6. **Proper Training:** In order to bring firmness in the changed order, the concerned employees should be properly trained. They should be able to know new techniques and knowledge. The concerned employees should be given orientation training. The policy of positive motivation should be used.

7. **Sharing of Income:** The extra income desired from changes should not be taken away by the management only, but should be shared with all the employees.

1.8.6 Kurt Lewin's Force Field Analysis Change Model

Kurt Lewin's force field analysis change model was designed to weigh the driving and restraining forces that affect change in organisations. The 'force field' can be described as two opposite forces working for and against change. In this illustration we'll learn how to analyse the force field.

Force Field Analysis Change Model

Have you ever had that conversation with colleagues about where to dine for lunch? You and a few others want to try the new Thai place, but your co-worker Jeanie and a few others want to go to the same old sandwich shop you've been going to for years. Well, Kurt Lewin's force field analysis change model describes a similar situation.

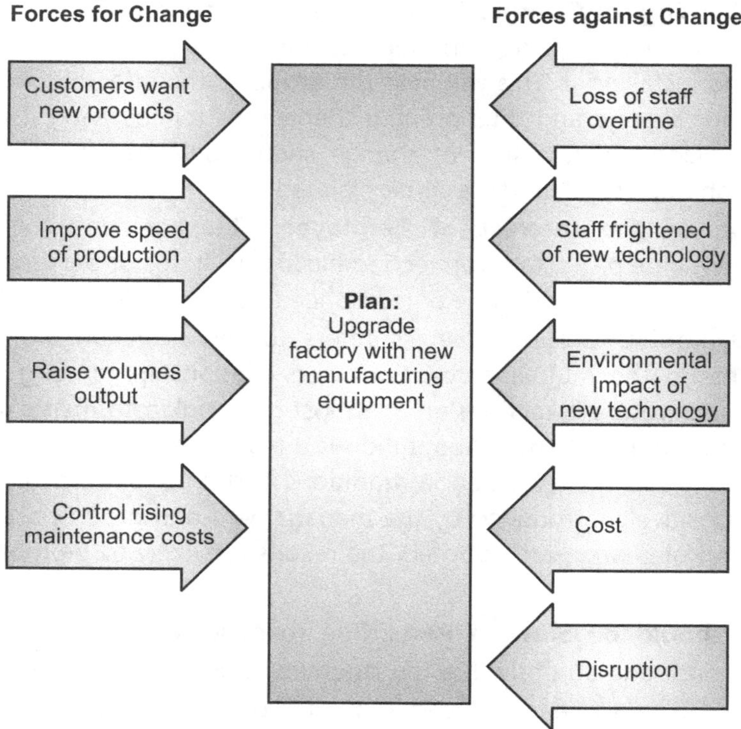

Fig. 1.2

The force field analysis is a method to:

- Investigate the balance of power.
- Identify the key players involved in decision-making.
- Identify who is for and who is against change.
- Identify ways to influence those against change.

In an organisation, change is a bit more complicated, but just like deciding where to go for lunch, there are driving and resisting forces at work. Driving forces are those seeking change. Resisting (restraining) forces are those seeking to maintain the status quo. The goal for the driving force is to gain equilibrium, or a balance of power. Resisting forces control the status quo, while driving forces seek change.

If driving forces exceed that of restraining forces, they will exact change. This will create equilibrium, or a balance of power.

Forces, whether driving or resisting, are a mix of:

- People
- Habits
- Customs
- Attitudes

How to Conduct a Force Field Analysis

The force field analysis involves:

- Stating the problem.
- Defining objectives.
- Determining resistant forces.
- Comparing strategy against organisational objectives.

In a Nutshell

Lewin's force field analysis change model works by investigating the balance of power, then determining the key players involved in decision-making and devising ways to influence them to accept change.

__Driving forces__ are those seeking change, while __resisting forces__ are those seeking to maintain the status quo.

The Force Field Analysis involves

- **Stating the problem** by determining the current situation in terms of the conflict at hand. This may also involve determining the desired state. Other things to consider are where the current situation will go if no action is taken.
- **Defining objectives** by listing the expectations or outcomes of change. If change occurs, equilibrium, or balance of power, has been achieved.
- **Determining resisting forces** to identify negative or resistant forces to change.
- **Comparing strategy against organisational objectives** to determine whether the strategies used are in line with the desired objectives.

A classic model of Organisational Development, commonly referred to as the 'force field' model, was proposed by Kurt Lewin in 1951. He described organisations as systems which are held in a constant state of 'equilibrium' by equal and opposing forces. The model suggests that a range of 'driving forces', which exert a pressure for change, are balanced by a number of opposing 'resisting forces'. Driving forces urging change might include the availability of new technology, economic pressure from competitors or even changes in local or national legislation. Conversely, resisting forces might include a firmly established organisational culture and climate or industry-specific customs. **Lewin** proposed that any process of organisational change can be thought of as implementing a move in the equilibrium position towards a desired or newly established position.

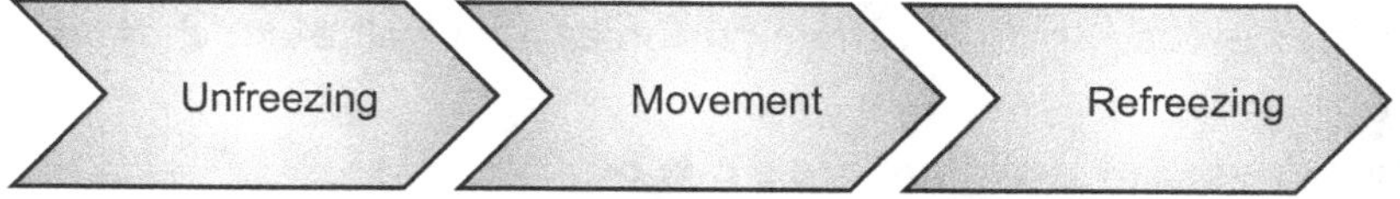

Fig. 1.3: Lewin's Three Stage Change Model

To elaborate on his model, **Lewin** also suggested a three-stage process of change implementation which is necessary for effective change within an organisation. Those three stages are:

- **Unfreezing:** Change efforts to overcome the pressures of both individual resistance and group conformity.
- **Driving Forces:** Forces that direct behaviour away from the status quo.
- **Restraining Forces:** Forces that hinder movement from the existing equilibrium.
- **Refreezing:** Stabilising a change intervention by balancing driving and restraining forces.

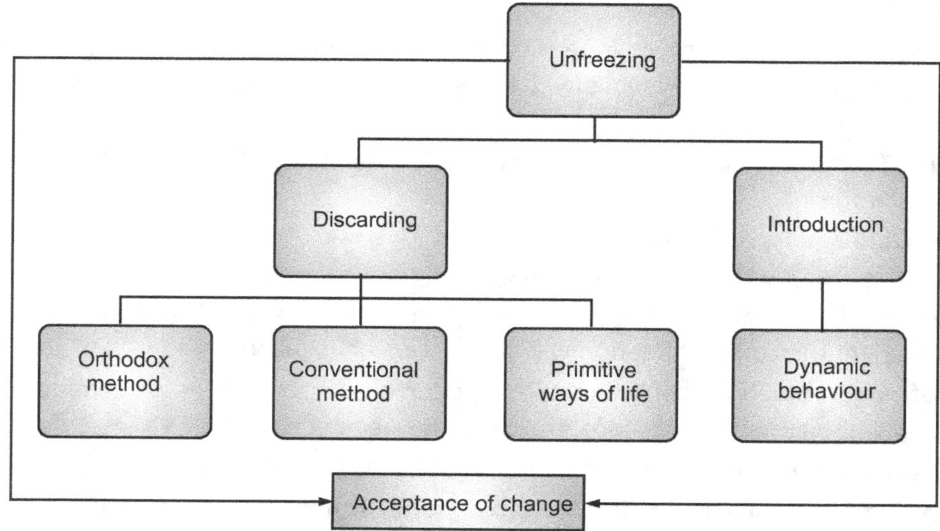

Fig. 1.4

An organisation must be prepared for any change which is about to occur. This process is known as 'unfreezing' and involves the investigation of resisting forces.

Any premature unilateral or authoritarian increase in driving forces for change will, according to the Lewin's model, be met by an equal and opposite increase in resisting forces.

No change will occur unless there is motivation within the organisation to do so. If there is no motivation, it must be induced. This is often the most difficult part of any change process.

Change not only involves learning, but unlearning something that is already present and well integrated into the personality and social relationships of the individuals. It is for this reason that an organisations culture can often act as a resisting force to change.

For a change to become routine and accepted into the day-to-day practices of an organisation, the organisation must go through the final stage of refreezing the organisational system. A variety of strategies may be adopted to achieve this, including new rules, regulations and reward schemes to reinforce the change process and maximise the desired behaviours of staff or employees.

1.9 STRESS MANAGEMENT

1.9.1 Definitions of Stress

1. According to **(Cox, 1985):** *"Stress is part of a complex and dynamic system of transaction between the person and his environment."*
2. According to **(Holroyd & Lazarus, 1982):** *"Psychological stress requires a judgment that environmental and/or internal demands exceed the individual's resources for managing them."*
3. According to **(Eliot, 1988):** *"Stress may be viewed as the body's response to any real or imagined event perceived as requiring some adaptive response and/or producing strain."*
4. According to **(Humphrey, 1992):** *"In essence, stress can be considered as any factor, acting internally or externally, that makes it difficult to adapt and that induces increased effort on the part of the person to maintain a state of equilibrium both internally and with the external environment."*
5. According to **(Levi, 1996):** *"Stress is caused by a multitude of demands (stressors), such as an inadequate fit between what we need and what we are capable of, and what our environment offers and what it demands of us."*

1.9.2 Sources of Stress

1. **Workplace Stress :**

   There are multiple sources to get workplace stress.

   - **Long hour :** Due to hectic schedule and long hours, people can get stress especially ladies who has to handle family responsibility with domestic work.

- Long hours can disturb personal life if quality time does not spend with family. Many of the time it becomes a serious issue and effects are seen on children if they are not given time
- **Unfairness :** Unfairness, unequa; treatment among employees can create stress on employees which demotivate them to come to the office.
- **Lack Of acknowledgments and reward :** If organisation does not reward people who have worked hard and put their heart and soul in an organisation, it demotivate and create stress unnecessarily.
- **Little or No control on workplace activities :** If there is no control on workplace activities, and division of work is not done properly, it can create burdone on some employees which create stress. Overload or under workload both condition can create uneasiness among employees which leads to stress.
- **Lack of job security :** This is one of the main reasons why people are always seen under stress. Considering inflation and over demanding expenditures, along with uncertainties in job creates huge tension among people.
- **Office politics :** This is unwanted situations arises in the office due to many reasons. But the person who suffers from politics go under stress.

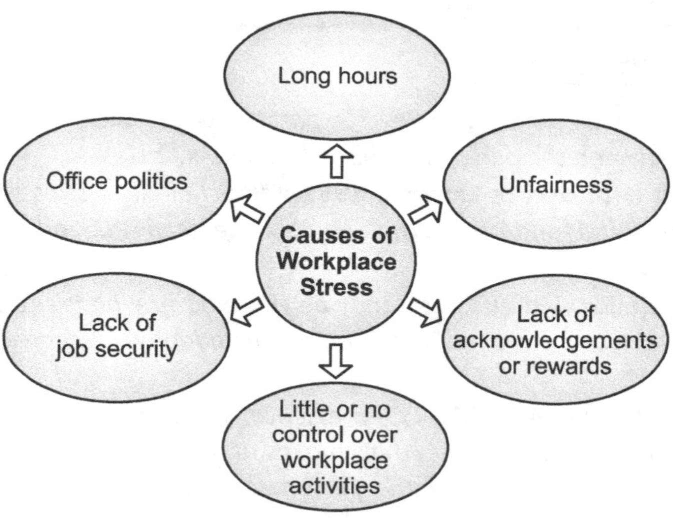

Fig. 1.5

2. Personal Stress:

While job stress is important to consider, stresses in our personal life can cause issues in our job.

- **Everyday challenges:** Getting caught in traffic or a leaky water heater would be examples of things that cause stress in our personal lives. Luckily, most of us have the abilities to cope with these daily stresses. However, too many of these types of stressors in one day can build up and cause major issues at work or in our personal life.

- **Personality:** Our individual personalities can impact our ability to handle stress. We are characterized two main personality types, type A and type B. People with a type A personality tend to be more time conscious, impatient, and preoccupied with tasks. A Type A Behavior Pattern (TABP) is characterized by impatience, aggressiveness, a sense of time urgency, and the desire to achieve recognition and advancement. People with a type A pattern may have a hyper awareness of time and, as a result, perform tasks quickly. Because of these patterns, the person with TABP may feel constantly rushed as they strive to be constantly competitive, causing stress and related health issues. Type A personalities are not viewed as a fixed trait but rather a set of predispositions that may occur in certain situations only. For example, Amiee may exhibit a type A personality at work but at home may not be as time sensitive and impatient. Type B personalities are more focused on the here and now and are much more laid back. Type B personalities do not normally experience as much stress as their type A counterparts because their viewpoint on time and achievement is different.

- **Work-life balance:** Everyone must manage multiple roles in their life. The roles of mother or father, boss, employee, spouse, sister, or brother have their own unique demands that can create stress at home and at work. When we have challenges at work, this can affect our roles at home and vice versa. Although many organizations promote a work-life balance and create a culture that allows people to have a "home life," easy access to send that "one last email" at 9pm for work creates a blurred line between home and work. This creates an even greater need for our emotional intelligence skills (self-awareness and self-management) in that we must be aware of our emotions and handle them when they come—rather than just going about our day and plowing ahead.

- **Life changes:** There are forty-three life changes that are characterized as creating stress. These life changes are measured on a scale called life change units, created by Thomas H. Holmes and Richard Rahe. The life changes are said to cause stress in one's personal life. However, personality type and situational factors may affect how much a particular event affects a person. For example, suppose a major life change such as the death of a spouse occurs. This would cause an immense amount of stress, but assume the spouse was very ill for a long period of time. In this situation, the latter could have caused stress as well. So while the scale has value in terms of determining what life changes cause the most stress, it is also important to consider the other factors around the life change, along with a person's personal coping ability.

- **Financial issues:** Tough economic times, combined with increasing costs of fuel and other living expenses, create great stress on individuals and families. Not having enough money to buy basic needs and lacking the ability to buy the wants we have can lead to anxiety, tension, and depression. These emotions can carry over into our work life, resulting in lowered productivity and lowered human relations with our coworkers.

- **Friends and family issues:** Challenges with family, in-laws, and friends create a great source of stress as well. While most of us depend on friends and family for support, tension and disagreements can cause stress.

1.9.3 Effects of Stress

Effects of stress could be seen on:

- Health,
- Workplace

Lets us see in detail.

Common Effects of Stress on Health :

Indeed, stress symptoms can affect our body, our thoughts and feelings, and our behavior. Being able to recognize common stress symptoms can help you manage them. Stress that's left unchecked can contribute too many health problems, such as high blood pressure, heart disease, obesity and diabetes.

On your body	On your mood	On your behavior
Headache	Anxiety	Overeating or undereating
Muscle tension or pain	Restlessness	Angry outbursts
Chest pain	Lack of motivation or focus	Drug or alcohol misuse
Fatigue	Feeling overwhelmed	Tobacco use
Change in sex drive	Irritability or anger	Social withdrawal
Stomach upset	Sadness or depression	Exercising less often
Sleep problems		

Stress Management of Body

If you have stress symptoms, taking steps to manage your stress can have many health benefits. Explore stress management strategies, such as:

- Getting regular physical activity.
- Practicing relaxation techniques, such as deep breathing, meditation, yoga, tai chi or massage.
- Keeping a sense of humor.
- Spending time with family and friends.
- Setting aside time for hobbies, such as reading a book or listening to music.

Aim to find active ways to manage your stress. Inactive ways to manage stress — such as watching television, surfing the internet or playing video games — may seem relaxing, but they may increase your stress over the long term.

And be sure to get plenty of sleep and eat a healthy, balanced diet. Avoid tobacco use, excess caffeine and alcohol, and the use of illegal substances.

Effect of Stress on Workplace

**1.	Poor Time Management:**

The positive side of stress is that it can jump-start your adrenalin and motivate you to perform your tasks more quickly in response to impending deadlines. An overwhelming workload, lack of peer support and too many demands at once, however, contribute to a sense of frustration and panic that there isn't enough time to complete the work. According to the authors of "Performance Under Pressure: Managing Stress in the Workplace," if these conditions routinely result in overtime or having to take work home, the stress of being unable to manage time efficiently can fuel employees' resentment toward the company as well as negatively influence their commitment and loyalty.

**2.	Strained Interactions and Relationships:**

Stress is a major contributor to job burn-out and strained interactions with peers and supervisors, says Bob Losvyk, author of "Get a Grip!: Overcoming Stress and Thriving in the Workplace." The combined feelings of helplessness and hopelessness generate heightened sensitivities to any and all forms of criticism, defensiveness, depression, paranoia about job security, jealousy and resentment toward co-workers who seem to have everything under control, short-fuse tempers, diminished self-esteem and withdrawal.

**3.	Lack of Focus:**

Stress affects your ability to remember things you already know, to process new information you are learning and to apply both to analytical situations and physical tasks that require concentration. When you are mentally exhausted from all of the worries, anxieties and tension brought on by a stressful environment or lifestyle, you are more easily distracted and prone to make costly, harmful or even fatal mistakes on the job.

**4.	Effect on Health:**

In addition to headaches, sleep disorders, vision problems, weight loss/gain and blood pressure, stress affects cardiovascular, gastrointestinal and musculoskeletal systems, says Richard Weinstein, author of "The Stress Effect." If you're not feeling well, you're not going to do your best work. Further, the amount of sick leave taken to rest and recuperate from stress-related illnesses often means that the work only accumulates during your absence and, thus, generates even more stress about how to catch up once you return.

1.9.4 Stress Management at Workplace

Get Clear on Requirements from Job:

A factor that contributes to job burnout is unclear requirements. If we don't know exactly what's expected from us, or if the requirements keep changing with little notice, we may find ourself much more stressed than necessary. If we find ourself falling into the trap of never knowing if what we are doing is enough, it may help to have a talk with our supervisor and go over expectations, and strategies for meeting them.

Stay Away from Conflict:

Because interpersonal conflict takes a toll on our physical and emotional health, and because conflict among co-workers is so difficult to escape, it's a good idea to avoid conflict at work as much as possible. That means don't gossip, don't share too many of our personal opinions about religion and politics, and try to steer clear of colorful office humor. Try to avoid those people at work who don't work well with others. If conflict finds we anyway, learn how to deal with it appropriately.

Effective Conflict Resolution Skills Are Key to Less Relationship Stress

Stay Organized: Even if we are a naturally disorganized person, planning ahead to stay organized can greatly decrease stress at work. Being organized with your time means less rushing in the morning to avoid being late and rushing to get out at the end of the day. Keeping yourself organized means avoiding the negative effects of clutter, and being more efficient with your work.

Be Comfortable: Another surprising stressor at work is physical discomfort. You may not notice the stress you experience when you're in an uncomfortable chair for a few minutes. But if you practically live in that chair when you're at work, you can have a sore back and be more reactive to stress because of it. Even small things like office noise can be distracting and cause low-grade frustration. Do what you can to ensure that you're working from a quiet, comfortable and soothing workspace.

Forget Multitasking: Multitasking was once heralded as a fantastic way to maximize one's time and get more done in a day. Then people started realizing that when they had a phone in their ear and were making calculations at the same time, their speed and accuracy (not to mention sanity) suffered. There is a certain kind of frazzled feeling that comes from splitting one's focus that doesn't work well for most people. Rather than multitasking, try a new strategy known as chunking.

Walk at Lunch: Many people are feeling ill effects from leading a sedentary lifestyle. One way you can combat that, and manage stress at work at the same time, is to get some exercise during your lunch break and perhaps take short exercise breaks throughout the day. This can help you blow off steam, lift your mood, and get into better shape.

Keep Perfectionism in Check: Being a high achiever can help you feel good about yourself and excel at work. Being a perfectionist, on the other hand, can drive you and the people around you a little nuts. Especially in busy, fast-paced jobs, you may not be able to do everything perfectly. But striving to just do your best and then congratulating yourself on the effort is a good strategy. Your results will actually be better and you'll be much less stressed at work.

Listen to Music on the Drive Home: Listening to music brings many benefits and can offer an effective way to relieve stress after work. Combating the stress of a long day at work with your favorite music on the drive home can make you less stressed when you get home, and more prepared to interact with the people in your life.

1.10　WORK LIFE BALANCE

Introduction :

Work-life balance involves a number of interdependent factors. Establishing a work-life balance is the art of implementing as many of these factors as possible in both areas without causing damage elsewhere. It is therefore important to know what exactly belongs to a healthy working life and a healthy private life, and how these elements are connected.

Factors listed below can also work together across other categories (e.g. the "social working environment" factor in work life and the "friendships" factor in private life can often be

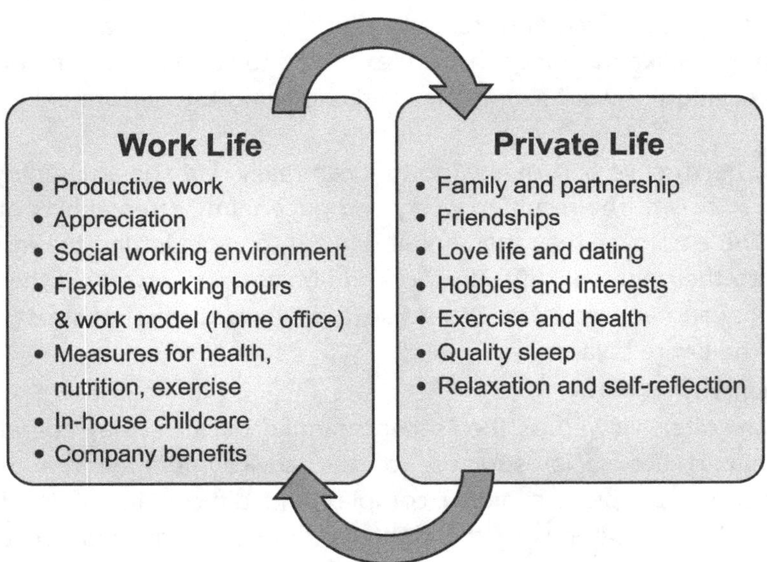

Fig. 1.6: Factors responsible for healthy professional life

For a healthy work-life balance, it is not only the relationship between the two sides that is important but also the individual factors of each side. When an employee drags problems into their work life or private life, the whole structure will suffer. On the other hand, personal issues can also have a negative impact on professional life. Clearly, a good work-life balance can only be achieved if certain conditions can be achieved within the workplace that ensure it does not stand in the way of the employee's happiness. Ideally, this happiness is the foundation and goal of a productive and healthy working relationship.

Productive Work:

For many employees, a satisfying professional life means that their own work brings visible and valuable results. In this sense, "productive work" does not mean maximum performance while disregarding other factors, but rather, the amount of valuable work that is optimal for each employee. For example, an unsatisfactory set of tasks means that an employee may not necessarily identify with their work and could therefore feel alienated from their work, which can ultimately have a negative effect on their work life.

Productive work consists of the right amount of both satisfying and fulfilling work. With the right conditions for productive work, the employer benefits from a high degree of motivation among employees. In contrast, unsatisfactory work may have a negative impact on one's private life if the employee takes that dissatisfaction home. A work-life balance therefore largely depends on the individual's quality of work and work satisfaction.

Appreciation of Work:

Here, the employer is particularly in demand. Most employees need a sense of appreciation both for themselves and their work in order to positively identify with the workplace. This appreciation should include both intangible rewards like praise, as well as tangible rewards like transparent promotion opportunities, fair salary, bonuses, etc. Most employees want to be perceived and treated with dignity. If a company ignores this point, it will treat its employees like machines that are expected to supply the same product over and over again. Appreciation of work simply means recognizing the performance of an employee and rewarding it.

A particularly destructive part of any job that can really damage an employee's happiness is unconstructive criticism. The resulting worry and uncertainty often affects other areas of an employee's life. The employee may then find it difficult to avoid letting the frustration of their work life seep into their personal life. The work-life balance only works if the employee feels treated with dignity and appreciation. Otherwise, a downward spiral of stress, frustration, and worry will shake the entire balance.

Social Working Environment:

Colleagues are often viewed as the "second family" because they spend so much time together. This makes the social structure of the environment all the more important. Relationships between people are highly complex and difficult to influence due to many individual factors. Nevertheless, with the right conditions, employers can ensure that the workplace becomes a breeding ground for interpersonal relationships. This includes a healthy interaction of clear hierarchies such as structures and social freedoms, clear rules against antisocial behavior like bullying and intolerance, team building measures, an "open office," and much more.

The right corporate structures, a positive corporate philosophy, and a corporate responsibility towards employees all create a good basis for employees to work not merely with colleagues, but rather with people whom they feel comfortable with. If an employee is poorly integrated into the social structure of the workplace, or if he/she experiences harassment or bullying, this can have devastating consequences on both the employee's professional and personal life. Here, both areas overlap; if the social work environment suffers, so too does the employee and therefore the problems seep into his/her private and professional lives.

Flexible Working Hours and Structures:

The term work-life balance is often understood to be a simple means of time management, but this is just one element of the work-life balance definition. However, the right timing is essential for the balance and provides the basis for many other factors.

In order to ensure that there is enough time for private or family life and working life, the employer has a number of options. On the one hand, home office is becoming increasingly popular, especially with so-called desk jobs. It affords employees the opportunity to work from home – all that is usually required is a functioning computer

A somewhat easier method for achieving this balance is with flexible working hours. The more freedom employees have with regard to their start and end times, break times, and the organization of weekly hours, the better they can adapt their professional life to their personal life. This is already the case in many workplaces, for example, it is often down to employees to decide when they begin and when they leave work, as long as they are fulfilling the required hours according to their contract. A general framework can be set (e.g. 8 hours between 7am and 8pm), and the more generous this is, the more flexible employees can be with their working hours. Many employers make Friday an exception to this framework so that employees can start their weekend sooner if they have already worked the full number of hours.

In-house Childcare:

Employees often have difficulty spending enough time with their children. The search for day care centers also presents working parents with serious challenges. This means that kids can upset the work-life balance greatly. On one hand, there are parents who spend too little time with their children because their work takes up too much time and attention. On the other hand, there are employees who, because of their obligations as parents, perform worse and are often absent.

Example : Volkswagen, an automobile industry has an effective solution to the above problems. Parents and children are then within a comfortable distance from one another. If a company provides the appropriate personnel and childcare facility, it can result in an inspiring, familiar atmosphere in the workplace. Generally speaking, in-house childcare is an effective way to help employees manage their work-life balance.

Company Benefits:

Company benefits can also have a positive impact on an employee's work-life balance. For instance, a company pension scheme defines how life in old age should be financed. Another popular company benefit is a public transport ticket, allowing employees to use public transport without incurring their own expenses.

Factors responsible for healthy private life:

The factors that contribute to a healthy personal life differ greatly from person to person. Everyone understands personal happiness to be something different. However, there are of course certain factors that play an important role in the personal lives of most people. If part of one's private life is unpleasant, this can often have direct consequences on one's professional life. Some employees have the ability to compensate an unfulfilled private life with a successful professional life. However, the following is probably true for most: a good work-life balance starts in your free time.

Family and Partnership:

Family is an essential part of leading a happy life. For most professionals, the end of a working day consists of time spent with family or a partner. If this time is stressful, the employee will not get the desired rest and a vicious circle of work and "work after work" begins to develop, which can eventually disrupt the entire work-life balance. In extreme cases, some employees will voluntarily do overtime at work in order to avoid going home. This, of course, also works the other way around: when the employee takes too much time for the family and endangers his/her job.

The exact elements of a good family life and a good partnership are very hard to explain. Nevertheless, the personal happiness of many employees is based on the strong support of their families. Both employees and employers have many opportunities to create good conditions for a full family life.

Friendships:

Many employees find it difficult (especially the older they get) to cultivate friendships outside of their professional lives. There are many reasons why meeting friends becomes more and more difficult with a full-time job. Firstly, many professionals are simply too exhausted after work for social activities, so friendships may therefore suffer. Secondly, a full-time job often leads to scheduling problems, especially if there is a family and kids involved.

Additionally, many workers tend to make their colleagues their new social anchor points that may previously have been filled by external friends. While this can often lead to a generally more pleasant working environment, it can also result in a friendship that is too heavily defined by the job itself. These friendships often end when the employment relationship ends. If the employee then neglected his/her external friendships, the employee may experience some social isolation.

Personal happiness, which helps forge a work-life balance, is often the result of longstanding friendships forming relationship anchor points outside of the workplace. This way, people do not feel reduced to a mere employee in the workplace. External friends are very important for one's own well-being because, to put it simply, they allow access to the world outside of the workplace. This is essential to the work-life balance, which is why friendship should never be underestimated.

Hobbies and Interests:

Most employees have a number of hobbies and interests that they want to pursue in addition to their jobs. However, many jobs make this considerably difficult. Certain hobbies that follow fixed schedules must sometimes be ruled out due to inflexible working hours. Additionally, a stressful job can often leave the employee too exhausted to pursue any interests or hobbies after work. Here, the individual's self-realization during leisure time is at stake – private life makes room for a demanding work life. The work-life balance suffers noticeably.

In addition to more flexible working hours, employers have several ways of valuing the individual interests of their employees. Internal social networks are popular platforms for the exchange of interests. This enables employees to network and arrange joint activities. Sharing hobbies and interests with colleagues has two key benefits: firstly, planning activities in a group means that others can work around your schedule, as opposed to an individual joining a class. Secondly, this strengthens the social dynamic within a workplace, because shared interests do wonders for relationships. However, it is also important to remember what has been said above on the subject of friendships.

Exercise and Health:

The topic of health affects all areas of a person's life and is therefore a central part of the work-life balance. Almost all factors – social, personal, family, psychological, or physical – are closely linked with health. Exercise has been proven to play an essential role in both physical and mental health.

Many employees seek balance through movement and exercise, especially because they spend most of their working life sitting down. With desk jobs it is particularly important to exercise for at least half an hour a couple of times a week. It is also advisable to be on your feet for at least five minutes for every hour you spend sitting. Physical fitness is important to most people, which is why sporting activities during free time are of great importance.

In addition to providing healthier working conditions (see above), companies can also ensure their employees lead a well-balanced life in terms of sports. Possible activities they can offer may include company runs, football tournaments, or fitness studio discounts. Ultimately, however, it is the employee's responsibility to ensure whether or not, and to what extent, they would like to partake in such offers.

Finally, it is of great importance that both the employer and the employee pay attention to the topic of health. This means, on the one hand, that employees take care of their health in their private time, and, on the other hand, that the employer is understanding towards sick employees and is obliging, to a certain extent, towards absences and medical appointments during working hours. This can prevent a sick employee from getting into a dangerous downward spiral.

Sleep:

An often underestimated factor of one's overall health is a healthy sleep cycle. Sleep deprivation can result in poor performance, mood swings, increased physical susceptibility, and many other risks. A person's sleep is often a good indication of their work-life balance status. It is therefore not surprising that many psychologists and doctors consider healthy sleep to be a key factor of a happy life.

Relaxation and Self-reflection:

This factor largely depends on how each individual perceives relaxation and how much of it they require. Many people enjoy a healthy professional and personal life, yet still struggle to find peace. Your life has the same flow every day: head to work in the morning, have lunch with colleagues, go home to your family after work, spend time with your partner and/or your children, exercise, and go to bed. What sounds like a good work-life balance can often feel somewhat superficial for the individual as they may feel like they never have time for themselves.

Advantages of a healthy work-life balance:

The aim of the work-life balance is to see that both employers and employees equally benefit from a work-life balance. The model must be adapted to each individual person. Nevertheless, some general benefits can be identified for both parties that have been proven in practice in many businesses. In the following overview, we outline the mutual interaction of a healthy work-life.

Advantages for employees	Advantages for employers
1. More importance is attached to one's private life and personal happiness.	1. The employee works more comfortably, more balanced, and more satisfied.
2. Flexible working hours make it possible for employees to better organize their private lives.	2. Which also makes the working time of each employee more effective.
3. A work-life balance encourages a healthier way of life.	3. Healthier employees are more productive, inspired, and satisfied.
4. Home office has a positive impact, especially on those with families.	4. Employer saves money and other resources with fewer people in the office.
5. Social events encourage more harmony between work and private life,	5. Social events also have a positive impact on team building.
6. Fitness offers and further training helps to develop the employee as a person.	6. This also leads to higher productivity in the workplace.
7. In-house childcare helps to keep work and family life in balance.	7. This makes it easier for parents to return to work after the birth.
8. A health-friendly working environment can increase the quality of work.	8. Happy employees mean increased performance.
9. Constructive feedback and transparent career development opportunities regulate professional life and alleviate private life.	9. Employer can better assess employees and communicate both praise and constructive criticism efficiently.
10. Sabbaticals are a great opportunity for employees to straighten out their work-life balance without risking their career.	10. Sabbatical helps retain high-performers in the long term, lowers the risk of burnout, and strengthens employees' identification with the employer.

1.11 QUALITY OF WORK LIFE (QWL)

Meaning:

Quality of work life (QWL) refers to the favourableness or unfavourableness of a job environment for the people working in an organisation. The period of scientific management which focused solely on specialisation and efficiency, has undergone a revolutionary change.

The traditional management (like scientific management) gave inadequate attention to human values. In the present scenario, needs and aspirations of the employees are changing. Employers are now redesigning jobs for better QWL.

The QWL as strategy of Human Resource Management has assumed increasing interest and importance. Many other terms have come to be used interchangeably with QWL such as 'humanisations of work' 'quality of working life, 'industrial democracy' and 'participative work'.

Definitions :

1. **The American Society of Training and Development :** "QWL is a process of work organisations which enable its members at all levels to actively; participate in shaping the organizations environment, methods and outcomes. This value based process is aimed towards meeting the twin goals of enhanced effectiveness of organisations and improved quality of life at work for employees. " -

2. **Nadler and Lawler :** "QWL is a way of thinking about people, work and organisations, its distinctive elements are (i) a concern about the impact of work on people as well as on organisational effectiveness, and (ii) the idea of participation in organisational problem-solving and decision making."

3. **Luthans :** "The overriding purpose of QWL is to change the climate at work so that the human-technological-organisational interface leads to a better quality of work life."

4. **Q.W.L. :** The sum total of physical (working conditions), psychological and economic factors which affect the job.

Objectives of Q.W.L.:

- To improve the standard of living of the employees.
- To increase the productivity of workers and of an organisation.
- To create a positive attitude in the minds of the employees.
- To increase the effectiveness of the organization (Profitability, goal accomplishment etc.).

Factors Responsible for Quality of Work Life

1. **Providing Job Security:** If an employee is confident that his job is secure, they are much more relaxed and can perform better. It gives them a confidence that even if something goes wrong by mistake, their job will not be at stake

2. **Rewards and recognition:** If an employee is awarded for a good performance, its helps them to perform even better. The leadership and top management must ensure recognition of the efforts of subordinates. This is an importance aspect of good governance as well.

3. **Flexible work timings:** Flexibility during working hours is something which is appreciated by employees. This gives employees a chance to do their work and also work on certain important personal commitments. This significantly contributes to improving the quality of work life for an employee. Companies also promote a compressed work week concept.

4. **Increased employee participation:** Involving employees in discussions, strategies & feedback is something which helps increase the employees QWL & contribution towards a particular role.

5. **Open communication:** Transparency between management and employees & effective team management gives them confidence as they are updated with the business and also feel at ease being approachable

6. **Career growth plans:** Discussing the future of the employee in the company, interesting aspects of the job, career development etc are all appreciated by employees

7. **Job enrichment:** Companies which are able to enrich the job with new tasks, better learning & training, more opportunities etc are more likely to keep employees happy at work.

Barriers to Q.W.L.:

- Resistance to change both by management and employees.
- There is a general perception that Q.W.L. implementation will cost much to the organization.
- Continuous increase in Q.W.L. may result in less productivity, i.e., after a certain level the productivity will not increase in proportion to the increase in Q.W.L.

Countries that Practiced Q.W.L.:

- Sweden
- Denmark
- Holland
- Switzerland
- Australia
- USA

Companies practicing Quality of Work Life:

- General Motors
- Ford Motors with UAW
- XEROX
- IBM
- BHEL, TISCO

1.12 TOTAL QUALITY MANAGEMENT

- The concept of TQM is of a very recent origin and developed after 1980.
- It deals with the product in its totality.
- It is a strategic total approach and comprehensive system of managing the entire organisational activities which result in the production of quality goods and services through constant innovation by doing the right things at the right time.
- It aims at a continual increase in consumers' satisfaction at continually lower cost.
- From this point of view, TQM is a continuous process of improvement for all employees and total organisation.
- TQM is a very wide concept which encompasses many aspects such as quality management, quality control, quality assurance, quality operations and continuous improvement, etc.
- In short, TQM means building, controlling and maintaining quality in everything and in every area. It needs collective efforts towards excellence.
- Quality circles, quality assurance, quality control, quality planning, are some of the important key elements of TQM.
- TQM is, in essence, a customer-oriented, quality focused management philosophy.

Features or Characteristics of TQM :

(a) Continuous Process :

- TQM is a continuous process.
- Constant and continuous efforts are required to improve the quality of goods produced and services rendered and also to reduce costs.

(b) Quality Management :

- Quality management is given importance in TQM approach which helps the organisation to face the challenges from the competitors and to meet the requirements of the customers.
- Reduction in costs helps to earn more profits.

(c) Focus :

- In TQM, the focus is always on the consumers.
- Making continuous efforts to satisfy the customers is an integral part of the TQM.

(d) Defect Free Approach :

- Defect-free approach as an integral part of TQM places emphasis on defect-free work.
- The idea behind it is to strive for perfection in the work.
- It definitely helps to improve and maintain the quality of goods.

(e) People-based Management :

- "People-based Management" is one of the principles of TQM.

- The management has to make its employees understand what they have to do and how they should do.
- Management should get the feedback about the performance of the employees.
- Management should make all the efforts to get the co-operation of its employees.
- If the employees are committed to customer satisfaction, they do their work with responsibility and efficiently.
- The quality is definitely influenced and improved by continuous involvement of the people working in the organisation.
- Thus, employees' involvement must be there in the TQM process.

(f) Reward :

- When the management expects their employees to work hard and sincerely, recognition and reward become an integral part of a TQM programme.

(g) Management by Fact :

- "Management by Fact" is another important principle to determine the quality of the product or service that the customers use and what they expect.
- The present quality level can be used as a benchmark to improve further.
- Fact-gathering is an essential aspect of continuous improvement. Decisions are taken on the basis of facts.

(h) Techniques :

- In TQM, various techniques such as quality circle, value engineering and quality control etc. are used.
- It becomes possible to improve systems and procedures through these techniques. Thus, TQM is a very wide concept.

(i) Responsibility :

- TQM, in fact, is the responsibility of the top management. However, the top management cannot do everything alone.
- Hence, there must be co-operation from the employees working at different levels.
- Therefore, requires it team-work to make TQM process successful.

(j) System Approach :

- TQM is a systems approach to managing the organisation and business and improving the performance.
- The systems approach begins with the commitment and effective leadership of top executives and their colleagues.

(k) Philosophy :

- TQM is necessarily a management philosophy which includes all activities through which the needs and expectations of the customers as well as the goals or objectives of the organisation are attained or achieved in the most effective and efficient manner by using the potential of all the employees for the further improvement.

1.13   CULTURAL DIVERSITY

- The globalisation of business, increased mobility of labour across geographic borders is leading to multiculturalism among several countries.
- For example, in countries such as Canada, US, UK, India, and Australia, multiculturalism is increasingly becoming an integral part of the national identity.
- In addition, cross-border mergers and acquisitions (e.g. Arcelor-Mittal) and deployment of teams for certain projects, require organisations to draw from a pool of human resources from different countries.
- The globalisation of the business environment that is being driven by technological and economic factors is resulting in an ever-increasing number of cross-cultural interactions in the workplace.
- Recent estimates indicate that there are over 1000,000 firms with international operations, and they have annual revenues in excess of $3500 billion.
- Not surprisingly, the growth in the number of firms with international operations has been accompanied by an increase in the cultural diversity of their employees.
- Much of our personal and interpersonal interactions are guided by cultural values, expectations, and attitudes.
- Some values transcend cultural boundaries and are mutually reinforcing.
- Other cultural values create interactions with high potential for conflict, misunderstanding, poor performance, and ultimately, individual and organisational ineffectiveness or failure.

Important Definitions of Multi-culturalism /Cultural Diversity :

(a) The Oxford Dictionary defines the word multicultural as "including of people of several different races, religions, languages and traditions".

(b) Multiculturalism is defined as "the presence of people from two or more cultural backgrounds within an organisation".

(c) Multicultural work force is "one wherein a company's employees include members of a variety of ethnic, racial, religious, and gender backgrounds whereas managing multicultural workforce goes further, and focuses on changing mindsets, organisation culture. It's strategy-driven and is seen as contributing to the organisational goals of profit, productivity and morale".

Points to Remember

- Organisational behaviour is directly concerned with the understanding, predicting and controlling of human behaviour in organisations.
- Organisational behaviour is built on the contributions from a number of behavioural sciences such as Psychology, Social Psychology, Sociology, Anthropology and Political Science.

- There are different models of OB. Some of them are still in practice while others have become outdated. These are: Autocratic Model, Custodial Model, Supportive Model, Collegial Model and System Model.
- Within an organisation there may be more than one model being practiced by different departments. Different managers may adopt different models according to their personal preferences.
- Approaches to OB are: Classical, Human Relations including neo-human relations, Systems, Contingency, Decision Making, Social Action and Postmodernism.
- Organisational change is a structured approach undertaken to ensure that changes are introduced smoothly and implemented successfully to survive in the evolving business environment and gain a competitive advantage over others.
- Change can be at individual, group and organisational level.
- The organisational changes are related to: People, Organisation, Systems and General Changes.
- Resistance to change is normal and people cling to habits and to the status quo. Managerial actions can minimise or arouse resistance.
- Reasons for resistance to changes include: Economic Causes, Personal Causes and Social Causes.
- There are some common best practices that can help to defeat resistance to change.
- Organisational Development is an effort that is planned, organisation-wide, and managed from the top, to increase organisational effectiveness and health through planned interventions in the organisation's processes, using behavioural-science knowledge.

Questions for Discussion

1. Define organisational behaviour.
2. "Behaviour is generally predictable, so there is no need to formally study OB." Do you agree or disagree with this statement? Why?
3. Discuss the models and approaches of OB.
4. What are the levels and types of change?
5. What are the sources for resistance to change? How can it be overcome?
6. What is stress? State its sources.
7. Explain the concept of work life balance.
8. Explain the concept of quality of work life.

Multiple Choice Questions

1. Organisational behaviour is ......
    (a) a science   (b) an art
    (c) a science as well as an art   (d) none of the above
2. The field of organisational behaviour examines factors such as the nature of leadership, effective team development and:
    (a) interpersonal conflict resolution; motivation of individuals
    (b) organisational control; conflict management
    (c) motivation of individuals; planning
    (d) planning; development
3. The term 'psychology' is derived from the ...... word 'psyche', which means 'soul' or 'spirit'.
    (a) Latin   (b) French
    (c) Greek   (d) None of these
4. The field of organisational behaviour is primarily concerned with ......
    (a) the behaviour of individual and groups
    (b) how resources are effectively managed
    (c) control processes and interactions between organisations and external context
    (d) both (a) and (c)
5. The study of organisational behaviour has certain basic assumptions. They are ......
    (a) an industrial enterprise is an organisation of people
    (b) these people must be motivated to work effectively
    (c) the goals of the employee and the employer may not necessarily coincide
    (d) all of the above
6. Scientists of OB recognise that organisations are not static but dynamic and ......
    (a) processing   (b) systematic
    (c) ever changing   (d) researching
7. Which of the following frameworks is used in the development of the overall model of OB?
    (a) The cognitive framework   (b) The behaviouristic framework
    (c) The social learning framework   (d) All of the above
8. Which of the following represents correct sequencing of historical developments of Organisational Behaviour?
    (a) Industrial revolution → Scientific management → Human relations movement → OB
    (b) Industrial revolution → Human relations movement → Scientific management → OB
    (c) Scientific management → Human relations movement → Industrial revolution → OB
    (d) None of these

9. Which of the following forms the basis for the autocratic model of OB?
    (a) Obedience   (b) Authority
    (c) Power   (d) Dependence on boss
10. "Might is right" is the motto of ......
    (a) Autocratic Model   (b) Custodial Model
    (c) Supportive Mode   (d) Collegial Model
11. Which one of the following is the definition given by Fred Luthans?
    (a) "Organisational behaviour is to understand, predicting and controlling human behaviour at work"
    (b) "Organisational behaviour is subset of management activities concerned to human behaviour"
    (c) "Organisational behaviour is a branch of social sciences that seeks to build theories"
    (d) "Organisational behaviour is a field of study that investigates the impact on behaviour"
12. Now days a lot of stress is being put on the ...... of the employee in the organisation.
    (a) character   (b) improvement
    (c) behaviour   (d) rewards
13. OB focuses on 3 Levels ......
    (a) Individuals, Organisation, Society   (b) Society, Organisation, Nation
    (c) Employee, Employer, Management   (d) Individual, Groups, Organisation
14. Scope of OB does not include ......
    (a) Leadership   (b) Perception
    (c) Job Design   (d) Technology
15. A manager with good ...... can make the work place more pleasant.
    (a) communication   (b) knowledge
    (c) experience   (d) interpersonal Skills

| **Answer to MCQ's** |

(1) - (c), (2) - (a), (3) - (c), (4) - (d), (5) - (d), (6) - (c), (7) - (a), (8) (d), (9) - (c),
(10) - (a), (11) - (a), (12) - (c), (13) - (d), (14) - (d), (15) - (d)

Project Questions

Organisational Behaviour Research Project

Select a topic that is a leadership, management or organisational topic that you are interested in or that may be of value to you and your classmates. Use the list of sample topics below. Research the topic thoroughly using valid, reliable sources from an online periodical. (You should have 8-10 articles about your topic. Spend a few days in the library working on this project.)

1. Provide an introduction to your topic which includes why this is an important topic, i.e. statistics, application to work etc.
2. Next define any terms.
3. The bulk of this paper will be the review of literature from your articles. Organise your paper according to topics and use headings (APA format) to complete this section.
4. Conclude your paper by summarising your findings.

Case Study

Tony had just finished his first week at Reece Enterprises and decided to drive to a small lakefront lodge for some fishing and relaxation. Tony had worked for the previous ten years for the O'Grady Company, but O'Grady had been through some hard times of late and had recently shut down several of its operating groups, including Tony's, to cut costs. Fortunately, Tony's experience and recommendations had made finding another position fairly easy. As he drove the interstate, he reflected on the past ten years and the apparent situation at Reece.

At O'Grady, things had been great. Tony had been part of the team from day one. The job had met his personal goals and expectations perfectly and Tony believed that he had grown greatly as a person. His work was appreciated and recognised; he had received three promotions and many more pay increases.

Tony had also liked the company itself. The firm was decentralised, allowing its managers considerable autonomy and freedom. The corporate culture was easygoing. Communication was open. It seemed that everyone knew what was going on at all times and if you didn't know about something, it was easy to find out.

The people had been another plus point. Tony and three other managers went to lunch often and played golf every Saturday. They got along well, both personally and professionally and truly worked together as a team. Their boss had been very supportive, giving them the help they needed but also staying out of the way and letting them work.

When word about the shutdown came down, Tony was devastated. He was sure that nothing could replace O'Grady. After the final closing was announced, he spent only a few weeks looking around before he found a comparable position at Reece Enterprises.

As Tony drove, he reflected that "comparable" probably was the wrong word. Indeed, Reece and O'Grady were about as different as you could get. Top managers at Reece apparently didn't worry too much about who did a good job and who didn't. They seemed to promote and reward people based on how long they had been there and how well they played the never-ending political games.

May be this stemmed from the organisation itself, Tony pondered. Reece was a bigger organisation than O'Grady and was structured much more bureaucratically. It seemed that no one was allowed to make any sort of decision without getting three signatures from higher up. Those signatures, though, were hard to get. All the top managers usually were too busy to see anyone and inter-office memos apparently had very low priority.

Tony also had some problems fitting in. His peers treated him with polite indifference. He sensed that a couple of them resented that he, an outsider, had been brought right in at their level after they have had to work themselves up the ladder. On Tuesday he had asked two colleagues about playing golf. They had politely declined, saying that they did not play often. But later in the week, he had overheard them making arrangements to play that very Saturday.

It was at that point that Tony had decided to go fishing. As he steered his car off the interstate to get fuel, he wondered if perhaps he had made a mistake in accepting the Reece offer without finding out more about what he was getting into.

Questions:

1. Identify several concepts and characteristics from the field of organisational behaviour that this case illustrates.
2. What advice can you give to Tony? How would this advice be supported or tempered by behavioural concepts and processes?
3. Is it possible to find an "ideal" place to work? Explain.

Chapter 2

Introduction to Human Resource Management

Contents ...

2.1 Introduction to Human Resource Management

    2.1.2 Concept of Human Resource and Personnel Management

2.2 History of Human Resource Management

2.3 Objectives and Scope of Human Resource Management

2.4 Importance of Human Resource Management

2.5 Functions of Human Resource Management

2.6 Organisation of Human Resource Management (Role of HR Manager)

    2.6.1 Personnel Department in Line Organisation

    2.6.2 Personnel Department in Functional Organisation

    2.6.3 Personnel Department in Line and Staff Organisation

2.7 Role of Human Resource Management

2.8 Challenges before Human Resource Management

- Points to Remember
- Questions for Discussion
- Multiple Choice Questions
- Project Questions
- Case Study
- Questions From Previous Pune University Examinations

Learning Objectives ...

- ➤ To understand what is meant by human resource management
- ➤ To study the importance of human resource in an organisation
- ➤ To know organisation of HRM
- ➤ To be aware of the role of HR managers at different levels

2.1 INTRODUCTION TO HUMAN RESOURCE MANAGEMENT

Today, we are in the first decade of the twenty-first century. In the last decade of the 20th century and during the first seven years of this century, it was found that there are various very rapid and unprecedented changes have taken place in different fields, sectors, both at the national as well as at the global levels. Globalisation of business has become important subject of very serious discussion in the national economic, trade and commercial policies and also in the corporate world. Because of continuously changing socio-economic, technological, political conditions, human resources managers have to face various problems in the management of their human resources. Really, human resource management has acquired a new dimension.

It is always said that the term 'Management' means, besides other things, to manage men tactfully. It shows how much important is the management of human resources. Though there are many other organisational functions such as materials management, production management, management of finance, marketing management etc., it is undoubtedly true that the management of human resource pervades all other organisational functions. But what is "Human Resource Management"? In order to understand the meaning, nature of 'Human Resource Management, we must know some important definitions on 'Human Resource Management' But, first let us try to understand the meaning of 'Human Resources, their importance etc.

Human resource management is the process of bringing together an organisation and its people to achieve organisational as well as personal goals. It is a comprehensive approach which brings success to the organisation with the help of people's skills, knowledge and abilities.

According to Decenzo and Robbins: *"Human resource management is a process consisting of four functions viz. acquisition, development, motivation and maintenance of human resources."*

According to Gary Dessler: *"Human resource management refers to the policies and practices one needs, to carry out the people or human resource aspects of management position, including recruiting, screening, training, rewarding and appraising."*

According to G.R. Agarwal: *"Human resource management is a process concerned with the management of human energies and competencies, for achieving organisational goals through acquisition, development, utilisation and maintenance of a competent and committed workforce, in a changing environment."*

According to Edwin Fippo: *"Personnel Management is the planning, organising and controlling of the procurement, development, compensation, integration and maintenance of people for the purpose of contributing to the organisational, individuals and social goals".*

According to Wendell French: *"Personnel Management is the recruitment, selection, development, utilisation of and accommodation to human resources by organisations. The human resources of an organisation consist of all the individuals regardless of their role, who are engaged in any way of the organisation's activities."*

Reference: *1. Edwin B. Fippo, Principles of personnel Management, McGraw-Hill, New York (4th Edition), 1976, P5*

2.1.1 Concept of Human Resource and Personnel Management

Human Resource Management:

- Human Resource Management is a bundle of diversified functions and includes the activities which manage all the human resources and develop them.

- It is a proactive function which takes care of present as well as future needs of an organisation.

- It is an ongoing process for an organisation that works at all the levels of management. It uses people's skills, knowledge and aptitude as a resource and boosts them to get the best out of them.

- It involves functions such as recruitment, selection and industrial relations.

- Employees are treated as an asset which is to be utilised for the benefits of an organisation.

Personnel Management:

- Personnel Management is concerned with people at the workplace and their interaction and relations with each other. It includes various functions and activities which are designed to achieve personal and organisational goals.

- It works as an auxiliary function and responds to the demands of an organisation. It contains daily operations or routine work and focuses on improving the efficiency of an employee by providing them the resources and by motivating them.

- Employees are treated as a tool which can be used for the organisation's benefit.

- It is looked as a cost centre which always needs to be put under control.

The American Society of Personnel Management [ASPA], the largest professional association in the field of management; changed its name to the Society for Human Resource Management [SHRM] in the year 1990 and since then, the term human resource management is gradually replacing the term personnel Management.

Distinction between Personnel Management and Human Resource Management:

Personnel Management	Human Resource Management
1. Personnel Management is concerned with the planning, organising, directing and controlling the personnel employed; to attain the goals of an organisation. In short, it is the management of employees employed in an organisation.	1. Human Resource Management refers to a set of programmes / functions / activities designed and carried out for maximising effectiveness of employees as well as organisations. Thus, it is the management of skills, knowledge, talents, abilities, aptitude etc. of human resources.
2. Personnel management is considered as an auxiliary function.	2. HRM is a strategic management function.
3. Employees are treated as a tool which can be purchased, used, replaced and utilised for organisational benefit.	3. Employees are treated as assets or resources to be used for the benefit of an organisation, the employees, their family members and the society as a whole, with mutuality of interests.
4. Employees in an organisation are treated as a 'cost centre' and hence, all efforts are made to control labour costs.	4. Employees are treated as a 'profit centre' and hence, expenditure is incurred to develop human resources considered as a capital investment for future utility.
5. An employee is paid for his services and hence he / she is treated as an 'economic man' in Personnel Management.	5. In Human Resource Management, an employee is treated as a complete human being i.e. a social, economic and psychological entity.

2.2 HISTORY OF HUMAN RESOURCE MANAGEMENT

(A) During the period of Industrial Revolution in the 1700, Machines were utilised widely, technology was geared up and jobs were fragmented. Workers got special jobs which created specialisation and lead to improved efficiency and speed in the work. But this approach left workers as Sophisticated Machine Tools. Organisation started concentrating only on making profits in less time without considering the workers' satisfaction aspect.

(B) The Industrial Revolution resulted in influx of a huge number of immigrants. Need to create employment for all the immigrants immerged and their recruitment and management gained importance. The period witnessed the rise of a special class of managers who were considered at a higher level than the less privileged employees. This newly developed system created a gap between the labour force and the bureaucrat or the management. With the passage of time, the gap grew wider and the condition of the lower class labours got deteriorated. As such, there was a pressing need for human resource management. The situation brought together the labourers to form Labour Unions.

(C) This resulted in increasing employees' power considerably in the 1800 -1900. The B.F. Goodrich Company was the pioneer in designing a corporate employee department to address the concerns of its employees. National Cash Register followed the suit in 1902, forming a separate department to handle employee grievances, record keeping, wage management and other employee-related functions.

(D) In 1913, the U. S. Department of Labour was formed to promote the welfare of employees.

(E) In the 1920s and 1930s, 'Hawthorne studies' had a deep impact on the productivity of organisations which advocated improving the physical work conditions for the employees. Due to this, there was a shift in focus from 'workers' efficiency' to 'efficiency through work satisfaction'.

(F) After the commencement of the *Wagner Act of 1935*, also known as the *National Labour Relations Act*, 1935, personnel managers started gaining importance. Organisations also witnessed the *Social Security Act* which insured people after their retirement. In 1938, the *Fair Labour Standards Act* accounted for minimum wages for labourers.

(G) Between the 1960s and 1970s, HRM achieved momentum after the commencement of several acts like the Equal Pay Act of 1963, the Civil Rights Act of 1964, the Employee Retirement Income Security Act of 1974 (ERISA, and the Occupational Safety and Health Act of 1970. These laws ensured employees' safety and protection of their rights. It was made sure there is no discrimination in any form against the workers or labourers. Laws related to disabled people were enacted to prevent discrimination of disabled workers under the Americans with Disabilities Act in 1990.

(H) Human Resource Management has been given various names throughout its extensive history. Since the time it is being recognised as a separate and important function, it was called as 'Personnel Relations', which evolved to 'Industrial Relations', then 'Employee Relations', and finally to 'Human Resources'.

Evolution of HRM in India

- In India during the early 19th century industrialisation was at its boom, which influenced the need of personal management. But there was no separate department to look after the problems of labours except welfare officers that too who care about women and children only.

- During the 1st World War there was usual growth for Personnel Management. The number of welfare officers was increased. During this period the women were recruited in large numbers as most of the men had joined military.

- The first phase of labour management came in 1920 in factories to handle absenteeism etc.

- Between 1920's and 1930's there were employers who cared for their employees wellbeing by themselves e.g. Tata Steel in Jamshedpur.

- During 2nd world war, the personnel management faced an improving stage because the government has to produce large war material then personnel department worked in full time basis.

- After independence the role of personnel management became inevitable in industries. It played functions like formulation of HR Policies, Collective Bargaining, Industrial Relations, etc.

- In 1930's the concept of personnel management has been converted to HRM, due to various reason like:

  o View point about doing works,

  o Legislative frame work,

  o Government policies,

  o Trade unions,

  o Concepts in management,

  o Change in economy.

- In 1990, government of various countries liberalised their policy due to which the human started moving from one nation to another. So the need for cross cultural perspective of HRM evolved. Due to this the recruitment became more specific and selection is based on talent regardless of nationality.

- In Table 1.1, the evolution of human resource management in India can be summarised as follows:

Table 2.1

Period	Development Status	Emphasis on	Status
1920 – 1930	Beginning	Statutory Welfare	Clerical
1940 – 1960	Struggling for recognition	Introduction of Techniques	Administrative
1970 – 1980	Achieving Superiority	Regulatory Conforming Imposition of standard on other functions	Managerial
1990s	Promising	Human Values	Executive

2.3   OBJECTIVES AND SCOPE OF HUMAN RESOURCE MANAGEMENT

It has been already made clear that the HRM is that part of management process which develops and manages the human resources of an organisation for maximising the effectiveness of employees as well as organisation. From this point of view, the basic objective of HRM is to ensure the availability of a competent and willing workforce to an organisation, the attainment or accomplishment of its goals. HRM also aims to meet the needs, values, dignity, etc., of employees and has due concern for the socio-economic problems of the community and the country.

The important objectives of HRM are listed below:

1. To create an able and motivated workforce and ensure its effective utilisation to accomplish various organisational goals.

2. To establish and maintain suitable and sound organisational structure in order to secure integration of employees and groups and to create desirable working relationship amongst them for increasing the organisational effectiveness. For this purpose, efforts are required to be done to create a sense and feeling of belongingness and team spirit by encouraging the employees to make positive and valuable suggestions.

3. To create a proper atmosphere to maintain high morale and to encourage a value system and environment of trust, mutuality of interests.

4. To provide training and education for developing the human resources.

5. To provide opportunities for participation, recognition, etc., and for a fair, acceptable and efficient leadership.

6. To provide attractive incentives, monetary benefits, social security measures and welfare facilities, various non-monetary rewards, benefits, etc., in order to ensure the retention of competent employees.

7. To adopt such policies which recognise merits and contributions by the employees.

8. To ensure that there is no threat of unemployment by instilling confidence among the employees regarding stability of their employment.

9. An organisation has to bear in mind its responsibility towards the society as a whole. The society may not desire to enforce reservation in hiring and the laws leading to discrimination affecting the society badly or if certain organisational decisions have some negative impact on the society, such decisions should be avoided. It should be the objective of an organisation to use the resources for the betterment of the society and the nation as a whole.

If we want to categorise the above mentioned objectives of HRM that can be done in the following manner:

(a) Personal objectives,

(b) Functional objectives,

(c) Organisational objectives and

(d) Social objectives.

In order to attain the various objectives stated above, HRM has to perform certain functions and undertake important activities. Not only all major and important activities in the working life of a worker from the time of his or her entry into an organisation until he or she leaves the organisation come under the purview of Human Resource Management; but many other activities, topics are also studied in HRM. Human resource planning, job design and analysis, recruitment and selection, training and development, performance appraisal, placement, assessment, proper motivation to the employees, maintenance of union-management relations, human resource accounting and audit, etc., are some of the important activities. This makes clear the scope of Human Resource Management, which is really very vast. The major topics, aspects which are generally included in the scope of HRM are shown in the figure given below.

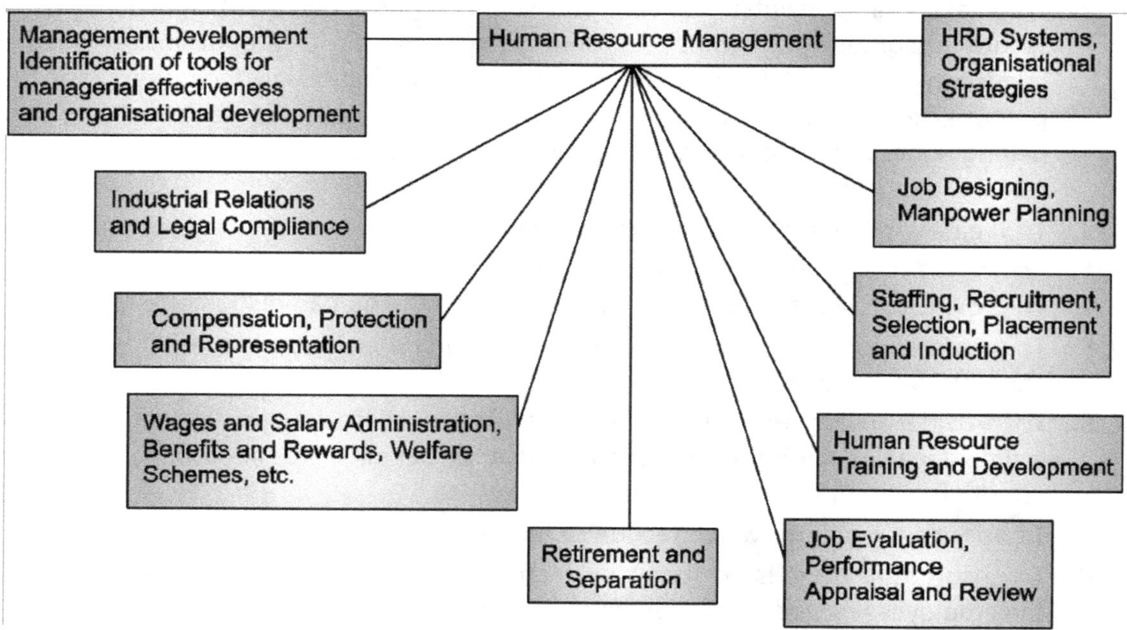

Fig. 2.1: Scope of HRM

Limitations of HRM

Human resource management is not only concerned about their department but it is an umbrella of other department. It has to care for every person from entry to exit in the company.

When the person grows in the company he naturally raises his skills and expertise. He also grows economically. But at the same time it creates load on company and on human resource department has to take care of his growing expectations along with keeping organisation satisfactory.

During this process, human resource managers faces many limitations at various ends.

Influencing factors of limitation of HRM

These are organisation, technical, Political, governmental, legal and economical etc. Let us see in detail

1. Organisational factors : Every organisation works into three levels like:

(a) Operational Level.

(b) Middle Level.

(c) Top Level.

Maintaining these levels and promoting people from lower level to upper level is the main task of human resource. This process is also called as Succession Planning. Succession Planning is not only promoting people to the upper level by position or by giving more responsibility but it also demand more hike in their packages.

In today's scenario, in every company, HR faces high labour turnover which is more expenditure on company's head. Human resource has to always keep a back up if any employee leaves and work suffers. They have to replace a person with same skill set into less or equal salary which sometimes become a very difficult task.

This and such situations are raising into every company nowadays. Keeping database ready, updating skill set of all employees so that replacement becomes easier. Online database hence a key point to the human resources where auto updation of database, or by manually through recruiters, agencies is done so that , finding out candidate from the database saves much of the companies cost.

2. Technical factors : Due to certain technical glitch, particularly in government or semi government sector, many time recruitment doest takes place. Example : In government college, Roater is an important register which many times does not get updated and due to which proper recruitment stops

Certain approvals from the government, document from the candidates, non compliance of the document like certain qualifications, transfer order etc. from candidates may create technical problem in recruitment, promotion or transfer.

3. Governmental factors : This generally applies to the area where recruitment is done through government. Many of the time appointment of such employees delays or replacement doesn't come easily, hence it burdons present manpower where human resource management has to play an important role. Extension of services, legal procedures, leave records, encashment, provident funds, transfers, arrears such and various situations cannot give liberty to the human resource department since they are legally bound.

4. Political factors : Due to political instability ,effects are seen on Human resource as well. Due to political influence and strategies, government makes the new rules and regulations which positively or negatively affect on business and ultimately this effects are seen on companies various operations. On recruitment and selection, if government puts some stays or hold on appointments of organization or private companies , this create huge impact on gaining talent, retaining employees across the border.

5. Legal factors : Some laws may displease the employees and if the displeasure increases, it will directly impact the performance of an organization.

The laws of an organization also decide how long the employees prefer to stick to the organization. Being an HR Executive, you must be able to assess the way in which each organizational law affects employees. The overall impact of the change in law and the ways to tackle the negative impacts should be gauged by an HR professional. These may include trivial laws related to break timings and leaves or serious laws regarding remuneration and bonuses. Every individual has a certain labour rights that give them security when they work in an organization. Every organization has to abide by these laws and rules and make sure that the workers get their basic rights while working in an organization.

6. Economic Conditions : One of the biggest external influences is the shape of the current economy. Not only does it affect the talent pool, but it might affect the ability to hire anyone at all. One of the biggest ways to prepare against economic conditions is to not only know what's happening in the world around, but also to create a plan for when there is an economic downturn. All companies can make due in a bad economy if they have a rainy day fund or plan to combat the harsh environment.

2.4 IMPORTANCE OF HUMAN RESOURCE MANAGEMENT

HRM plays a vital role in the organisation, at every level. It increases core competencies that distinguish an organisation from its competitors. The organisation can achieve its goals with the help of human resource, by utilising the available human resources with systematic planning and control.

- **At the Personal Level:** It helps in getting people with the best talent in the organisation. It also trains employees to explore more and facilitates the growth of their skills. It encourages people to work with commitment.

- **At the Social Level:** It gives status to the people due to their designation, facilities provided by the enterprise etc. It also provides enhancement in their career. The impact of fair wages and salary also brings satisfaction which results in their social aspects.

- **At the National Level:** It reduces unemployment which supports stable social development. Due to employability, people's enhanced skills, specialised education and change in attitude gives great benefit to the nation, by increasing the national income and GDP and leading to higher standard of living.

- **At the Organisational Level:** It follows the practices of pulling the talent and nourishing people for their and organisation's growth and development. It Increases the dignity of employees and also achieves success for the organisation by bringing in the talent. It also promotes work culture and increases productivity of an organisation. It formulates policies and strategies for the organisation.

2.5   FUNCTIONS OF HUMAN RESOURCE MANAGEMENT

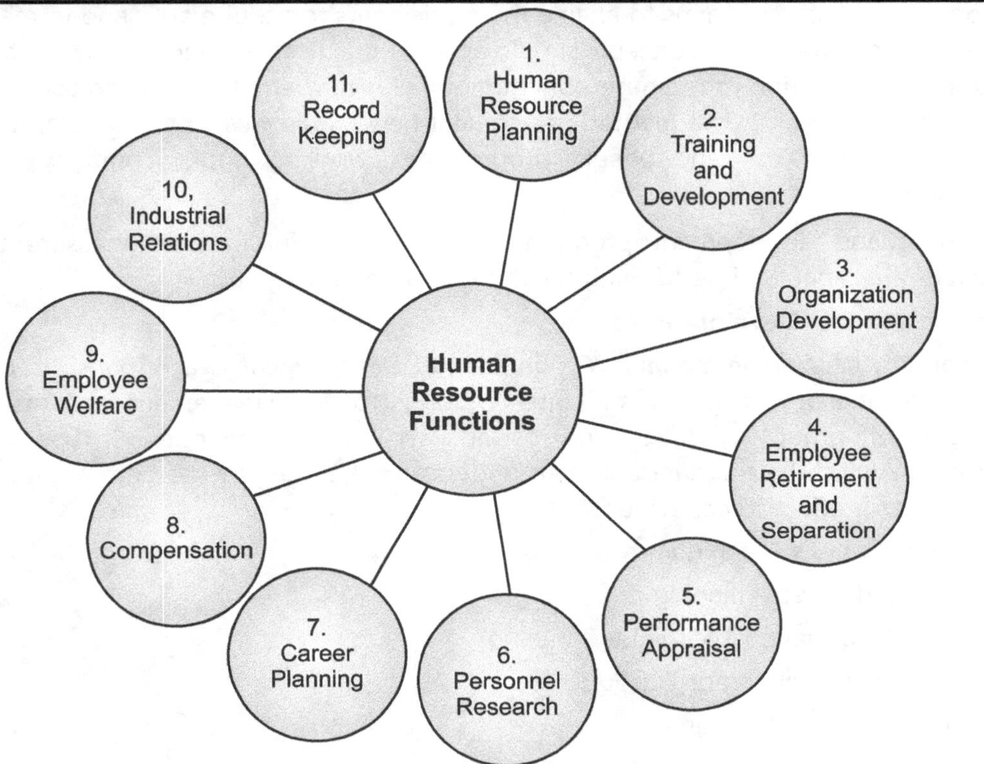

Fig. 2.2: Function of Human Resource Management

1.   Human Resource Planning:

This function creates a base for all the other functions carried out in an organisation. The number and type of employees needed to accomplish organisational goals are determined by this function. Research is an important part of this function because planning requires collection and analysis of information, to forecast human resources supplies and to predict future human resources needs.

The basic human resource planning strategy is staffing and employee development. It also requires job analysis which provides information about the nature of job, the number of employees required with specific skill, their responsibility, the salary amount for each position and the expected experience etc. It also involves preparing the job description. A job description spells out work duties and activities of employees and it makes employees to work as per the procedure. Job descriptions are a vital source of information to employees and managers, as job content has a great influence on personnel programmes and practices.

2.   Training and Development:

This function involves imparting the specific skills, education, abilities and knowledge to the employees.

Training is presumed to consist of some formal education. Any training and development programme aims to enable the participants to acquire skills and to make them understand how theoretical concepts should apply in practice. Training initially starts with an induction or orientation programme. Orientation helps new employees to adjust to the new job and the employer. It is a method to acquaint new employees with particular aspects of their job including pay and benefit programmes, working hours, company rules and expectations.

Training and development programmes provide useful means to assure that the employees are capable of performing their jobs at acceptable levels.

3. Organisational Development:

According to **Warren Bennis:** *"Organisational Development is a response to change a complex educational strategy."* It is an intervention in to the management structure so as to make use of group dynamics and social psychology techniques. It has following interventions which help organisations to understand their employees better and intend to change towards effective behaviour:

- Role Analysis Technique
- Life and Career Planning
- Role Negotiation Technique
- Sensitivity Training or T group
- Transactional Analysis
- Survey Feedback
- Life and Career Planning

4. Employee Retirement and Separation:

Most of the employees get separated from the organisation due to retirement. Organisation has to always make the retirement policies clear so that the employee can plan his life after retirement. The event of retirement is very important for the retiring employee. Hence HR manager has to arrange a farewell or a small programme to acknowledge his / her services to the organisation.

Retirement is of three types:
- Compulsory Retirement
- Forced Retirement
- Pre-mature / Voluntary Retirement

Separation: It is caused due to end of the employment contract or agreement or because of some special reason such as:

- Resignation
- Discharge
- Suspension
- Lay-Off

5. Performance Appraisal:

According to **Edwin B. Flippo:** "Performance Appraisal is a systematic, periodic and so far as humanly possible, an impartial rating of an employee's excellence in matters pertaining to his present job and to his potentialities for a better job."

According to **Afford Beatty:** "Performance Appraisal is the evaluation or appraisal of the relative worth to the company of a man's services on his job."

The objectives of the performance appraisal are:

- To evaluate the worth of an employee's skills and abilities to the organization.
- To improve supervision.
- To prepare compensation plans.
- To plan for suitable training and development programme.
- To give feedback on employee's performance.
- To offer promotions or change in job.
- To provide motivation to employees in the form of recognition of their work.
- To provide incentive to all the employees.

6. Personnel Research:

In a good research approach, the objective is to get facts and specific information about personnel in order to develop and maintain a programme that works. It is impossible to run a personnel programme without pre-planning and post-reviewing. There is a wide scope for research in the areas of recruitment, employee turnover, terminations, training and so on. Through a well-designed survey, employees' opinions can be gathered on wages, promotions, welfare services, working conditions, job security, leadership, industrial relations etc. However despite of its importance, in most companies, research is the most neglected area because human resource is too busy in solving the HR related issues. Research helps in preventing such issues.

7. Career Planning:

Each employee would like to stay in an organisation which provides him with a continuous career growth. Hence it is a responsibility of HR managers to do the career planning of all employees and to look after their growth in the organisation. Career planning activities include assessing an individual employee's potential for growth and advancement in the organisation.

8. Compensation:

Human resource personnel provide a rational method for determining how much employees should be paid for performing certain jobs. Compensation is a major cost to many organisations and hence it needs a careful consideration in human resource planning. Compensation levels affects staffing as people are generally attracted towards organisations offering a higher level of pay in exchange of the work performed. It is also related to employee development as it provides an important incentive in motivating employees to achieve higher levels of job performance and to get higher paying jobs in the organisation.

9. Labour Welfare:

Employee welfare includes various services, benefits and facilities offered to employees by the employers. It can be in any form; either monetary or non-monetary. This includes items such as allowances, housing, transportation, medical insurance and food. Employee welfare also includes monitoring of working conditions, creating harmony through establishing infrastructure for health, and providing insurance against disease, accident and unemployment for the workers and their families. Through such generous benefits the employer makes the standard of living better for employees.

10. Industrial Relations:

This is concerned with managing the relationship between the management and workers and playing the role of regulatory mechanism in resolving any industrial disputes.

It covers collective bargaining, which is a mechanism for resolving industrial disputes and grievances, setting disciplinary policy and practice, looking into legal aspects of labour etc. IR is acknowledged differently e.g. some term them as class conflicts and some term them as mutual cooperation's. HR manager is expected to understand these various understandings by applying different approaches to them like Unitary Approach, Pluralistic Approach and Marxist Approach.

11. Record-keeping:

The most basic function of HRM is employee's record-keeping. This function involves recording, maintaining and retrieving employee related information for a variety of purposes. Records which must be maintained include application forms, health and medical records, employment history, seniority lists, earnings, hours of work, absences, turnover and other employee data. Complete and up-to-date employee records are essential for most personnel functions. Employees today have a great interest in their personnel records more than ever.

2.6   ORGANISATION OF HUMAN RESOURCE MANAGEMENT

It involves:
1. Personnel department in Line Organisation
2. Personnel department in Functional Organisation
3. Personnel department in Line and staff Organisation

2.6.1 Personnel Department in Line Organisation

Line structure is very common in small firms. In this structure the authority flows from supervisors to subordinates. Every person knows who he has to report to and whom to issue orders. Line managers know fully about their responsibilities and the operations of their areas. One person - one boss principle is followed in this type of organisation.

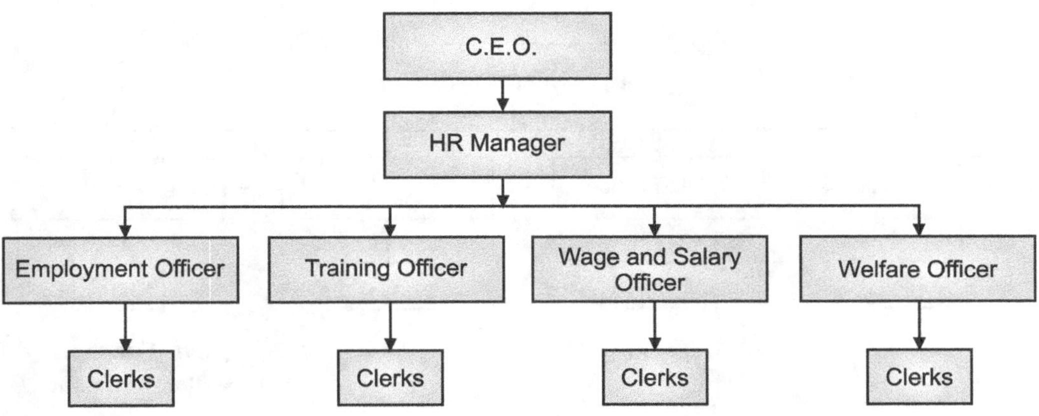

Fig. 2.3

2.6.2 Personnel Department in Functional Organisation

In this type all the activities are divided into various functions such as production, logistics, marketing, human resources and finance. This type of organisation brings more efficiency due to specialisation in the niche areas. It has a great advantage of clarity. It also reduces duplication and wastages.

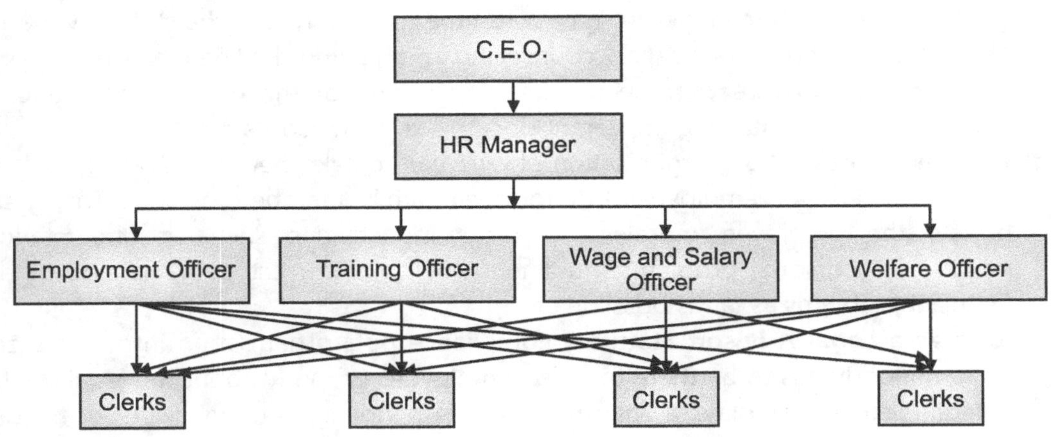

Fig. 2.4

2.6.3 Personnel Department in Line and Staff Organisation

This type focuses on line as well as functional type of organisation. Staff positions are created to assist line managers. This department offers more help and advice on personal issues to all the departments, without disturbing the unity of command principle.

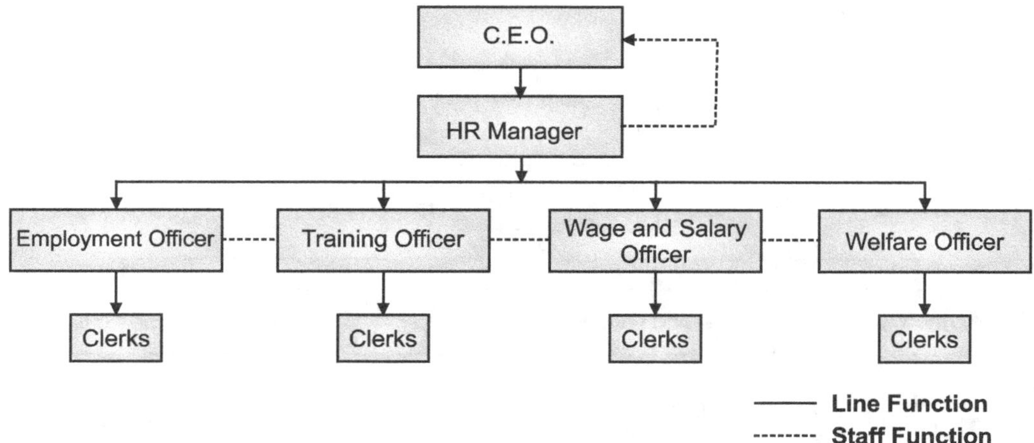

Fig. 2.5

2.7 ROLE OF HUMAN RESOURCE MANAGEMENT (ROLE OF HR MANAGER)

It includes:

(a) Role as a Policy Maker: One of the important aspects of any organisation is making policies towards achievement of its goals. Policy made by the administrator has to be followed by managers and employees.

(b) Role as an Advisor: One of the main responsibilities of personnel manager is to guide line and staff manager from time to time to comply with the statutory matters. Their main functions are guiding, counselling and helping the line managers

(c) Role as a Record-keeper: Record keeping is one of the routine level functions which includes maintaining important documents and records etc.

(d) Role as a Counsellor: Organisation always has to take new steps which not only shows concern for employees but for their family members as well. This greatly boosts the employee morale and includes activities such as understanding employees' personal problems, guiding them on a correct path, helping in their financial problems as far as possible etc.

(e) Role as a Legal Advisor: Statutory compliance puts organisation into a safe zone but somebody has to be there to guide employees properly about the legal matters. Personnel manager plays a role in grievance handling, settling disputes, handling disciplinary matters, collective bargaining, implementation of various laws, civil courts etc.

Routine level operations are carried through subordinates and need to be monitored closely by their supervisors. In such cases personnel managers can act as a recruiter, coordinator, mediator and trainer. The operational role of HRM involves:

1. **Procurement:** Planning, recruitment and selection, induction and placement.

2. **Development:** Training, development, career planning and counselling.

3. **Compensation:** Wage and salary determination and administration.

4. **Integration:** Integration of human resources with organisation.

5. **Maintenance:** Sustaining and improving working conditions, retentions, employee communication.

6. **Separations:** Managing separations caused by resignations, terminations, lay offs, death, medical sickness etc.

(a) Right strategies need to be designed by the top level managers, to get success in administration and operational activities. HR manager acts as change agent and makes sure that change initiative focuses on creating high performance teams, reducing cycle time for innovation or implementing new technology.

(b) Strategic HR does not stop at performing their administrative responsibilities only. Further their main task is to participate in corporate strategy rather than supporting administration.

(c) Strategic HR is more proactive rather than reactive in its relationships with the other functional areas. They do not wait for instructions, requisition or complaints but take actions before that.

(d) It is concerned about understanding future needs of its internal customers to compete globally.

(e) It does its homework, does research on the future and offers proactive solutions and strategic advice.

(f) Strategic HR is preventive rather than corrective. It is developmental in orientation.

(h) It views employees as resources, which should not be wasted but developed.

(i) Strategic HR aims to create a working environment conducive for employees to do things right at first time. It aims to prevent mistakes rather than punishing them.

Areas in which Human Resources can be of assistance: As the human resource is the heart of the department without this no function can go smoothly. As mentioned in above it plays various roles but as what position, this will get cleared from this point.

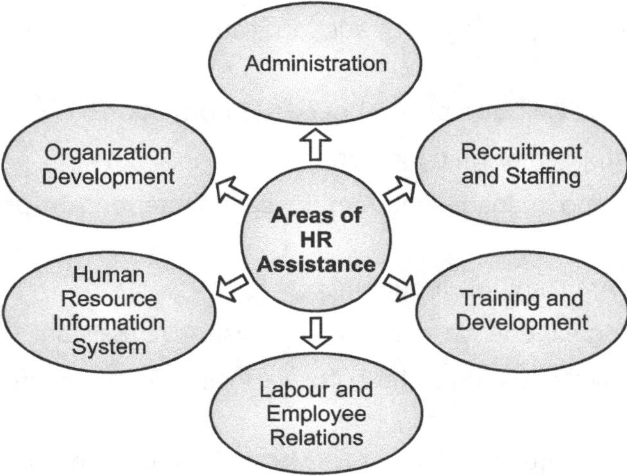

Fig. 2.6: Areas of HR assistance

HR has to plays an important role in

1. Administration : HR Administrative Assistant job profile:

Human Resources (HR) Administrative Assistants support management-level staff and perform a variety of tasks. The primary duty of an HR Administrative Assistant is to collect and manage all data pertaining to a business' employees, but they are also involved in recruiting, hiring, and training of new employees.

In order to attract HR Administrative Assistant that best matches your needs, it is very important to write a clear and precise HR Administrative Assistant job description.

HR Administrative Assistant job description:

If you are passionate about HR operations and you would like to give your contribution in creating a great company culture, this is the right position for those people this role will provide support the work of HR department by performing a variety of tasks. In this position, primary duty will be to collect and manage all data pertaining to a business' employees, sometimes also be involved in the recruiting, hiring, and training of new employees with regards to their documentations and filling

HR Administrative Assistant job duties and responsibilities:

- Provide administrative support for HR executives.
- Organize, compile, update company personnel records and documentation.
- Manage and update HR databases with different information such as new hires, terminations, sick leaves, warnings, vacation and days off.
- Help in payroll management, preparation and payment.
- Prepare, manage and store paperwork for HR policies and procedures.
- Answer employees' questions and provide requested information.
- Maintain schedule and coordinate calendar activities.
- Assist recruiters in posting job ads on careers pages and processing received resumes.
- Answer telephone calls and provide needed information.
- Create reports for senior management.
- Help organize and manage new employee orientation, on-boarding, and training programs.

HR Administrative Assistant job requirements:

- Previous working experience as an HR administrative assistant for (x) years.
- Ability to effectively use computer software including Microsoft Outlook, Word, Excel and HR software.
- Knowledge of HR software (HRIS or HRMS and Recruitment Marketing platforms).
- Familiarity with labour laws.

- Excellent organizational and time-management skills.
- Act as a reliable and supportive team member.
- BS in human resources or similar relevant field.
- Excellent communications and interpersonal skills.
- Data-driven mindset.
- Experience with recruitment marketing.

2. Recruitment and Staffing :

Recruiting employees whose talents are aligned with business goals is critical to the success of an organization. As such, human resources recruiters are highly valued in virtually all organizations and businesses.

Simplest terms, human resources recruiters develop and implement recruiting plans and strategies designed to fulfill company staffing needs.

As part of a human resources team, recruiters (also known as corporate recruiters and internal recruiters) are responsible for leading staffing efforts of a company and building a strong workforce that adds to the company's bottom line. These highly skilled and often equally highly educated HR professionals possess knowledge of employment and labor law, have a deep understanding of the organization and its staffing needs, and possess strong interpersonal and communication skills.

Most organizations view recruiters as being responsible for the entire recruiting cycle. In other words, these professionals are called upon to find potential candidates, screen them, and recommend them for placement. The process of recruiting may involve both internal and external sourcing methods, thereby requiring these HR professionals to be adept at understanding where and how to locate candidates.

Daily Job Duties of HR Recruiting Specialists:

The recruiting, interviewing, and screening responsibilities of HR recruiters can be further broken down by daily job duties, which include:

- Partnering with hiring managers to determine staffing needs.
- Screening resumes.
- Performing in-person and phone interviews with candidates.
- Administering appropriate company assessments.
- Performing reference and background checks.
- Making recommendations to company hiring managers.
- Coordinating interviews with the hiring managers.
- Following up on the interview process status.
- Maintaining relationships with both internal and external clients to ensure staffing goals are achieved.

- Communicating employer information and benefits during screening process.
- Staying current on the company's organization structure, personnel policy, and federal and state laws regarding employment practices.
- Serving as a liaison with area employment agencies, colleges, and industry associations.
- Completing timely reports on employment activity.
- Conducting exit interviews on terminating employees.

3. Training and Development :

As the workplace evolves with some advancement always, human resource training department always have to make sure updation of such technology and global business practices imparted among their employees, continual training remains a major focus of organizations and businesses across the country. Therefore, corporate trainers continue to be some of the most sought-after professionals in human resources.

Corporate trainers are focused on the planning, scheduling, and administration involved with training professionals in a corporate business environment. These professionals play an important role in the transition of new employees into the workplace, thus allowing them to become productive and efficient members of the corporate environment.

Corporate trainers also often conduct ongoing employee training for current employees. Therefore, their work often extends to facilitating the introduction of new technology or policies to a company's employees.

Although the most obvious aspect of a corporate trainer's job involves the actual training process, these HR professionals actually spend a considerable amount of time planning, organizing, and improving training programs, which consists of selecting and revising curricula.

Training specialists are responsible for developing and conducting training programs for new and existing employees, which includes the following duties and responsibilities:

1. Consulting with management and supervisors to stay current on organization policies, procedures, business initiatives, technologies, and regulations.
2. Coordinating corporate training programs with hiring and training periods and events.
3. Formulating curricula and instructional delivery methods as to accommodate hiring and training requirements.
4. Overseeing the creation and development of instructional training methods, such as individual training, group training, lectures, demonstrations, conferences, and workshops.
5. Selecting teaching aids that assist in training, such as handbooks, demonstration models, multimedia visual aids, webinars, and computer tutorials, among others.

6. Testing trainees as to measure progress and effectiveness of training programs.

7. Reporting on employee training progress to department management and supervisors.

8. Maintaining accurate training records.

9. Receiving feedback from employees regarding effectiveness of training methods.

4. Labour and Employee Relations :

The job description for a labor relations specialist includes the following duties/responsibilities:

1. Developing labor policies.
2. Negotiating collective bargaining agreements with the union.
3. Managing grievance procedures.
4. Looking into dispute resolution involving employees, management, unions, government agencies, other firms, etc.
5. Advising management on issues regarding union-management relations, such as contract negotiations.
6. Advising the HR staff to ensure compliance with the union contract.
7. Consulting with members of the executive HR staff regarding personnel policies.
8. Developing and revising union contracts.
9. Meeting with elected union officials.
10. Leading monthly labor management meetings.
11. Preparing paperwork related to labor relations assignments.

Labor relations specialists spend much of their time reporting to and working alongside the director of industrial relations in many corporations. These HR professionals also often seek the guidance and advice of conciliators (mediators) when attempting to prevent or resolve disagreements over contracts and other issues.

In governmental agency settings, labor relations specialists can be found working at the municipal, state, and federal levels. Although their work involves much of the same duties as those found in private companies or organizations, specific issues often involve job classification and other matters that are unique to a government setting. Labor relations specialists may serve government agencies as consultants and researchers, focusing their efforts on issues related to:

- Wages/hours
- Fair employment practices
- Safety codes
- Employer-employee relationships
- Unemployment statistics
- Labor laws
- Economics

5. Human Resource Information System (HRIS):

A HRIS, which is also known as a human resource information system or human resource management system (HRMS), is basically an intersection of human resources and information technology through HR software. This allows HR activities and processes to occur electronically.

To put it another way, a HRIS may be viewed as a way, through software, for businesses big and small to take care of a number of activities, including those related to human resources, accounting, management, and payroll. An HRIS allows a company to plan its HR costs more effectively, as well as to manage them and control them without needing to allocate too many resources toward them.

In most situations, a HRIS will also lead to increases in efficiency when it comes to making decisions in HR. The decisions made should also increase in quality—and as a result, the productivity of both employees and managers should increase and become more effective.

6. Organisational Development:

Overall development of an organisation is based on people's development which is the main responsibility of the HR department. Personal development through motivation, counselling is also one of the tasks HR has to do.

Skill enhancement program can run, technical training can be provided time to time which makes everyone confident and make achieve organisational goal.

2.8 CHALLENGES BEFORE HUMAN RESOURCE MANAGEMENT

There are many challenges before human resource management. Some are listed below:

(a) **Finding the Right Talent:** For running any business, finding right people with right attitude is very important but is an equally difficult task. HRM does not want to waste its valuable time in interviewing thousands of potential candidates who are not fit for its organisation. In today's time, finding the right talent has become a challenging task.

(b) **Managing Labour and Benefit Costs:** Managing diversified labour and employees with their demands has become tricky. Most companies, in such case, first reduce benefits of employees and cut down the staff. Employees who retain their jobs often end up working harder for getting less in terms of health insurance and paid time off. This can discourage entire staff-reducing employee productivity and leading to greater turnover. However organisation needs to maintain the profit margin with their employees.

(c) **Maintaining Work Culture:** Due to globalisation and diversity, organisation is required to maintain healthy environment for all.

(d) Managing Low Attrition Rate: More competition leads to high attrition. There is an opportunity for the HR manager to play safe and introduce good retention strategies.

(e) Economical and Technological Change: Changing economy has immense impact on the organisations. Also to adopt latest technology, recruit people with required skills or train them as per organisational requirements all the time, is costly as well as time consuming process. Human resource department always has to be ready with their back up of the employees who can complete the expectations of the organisation.

Points to Remember

- Human resource management refers to the policies and practices one needs to carry out the people or human resource aspects of management including recruiting, screening, training, rewarding and appraising.

- Personnel management is concerned with two sets of functions, namely managerial and operative.

- Human Resource Management has been given various names throughout its extensive history such as 'Personnel Relations', which evolved to 'Industrial Relations', then 'Employee Relations', and finally to 'Human Resources'.

- **Functions of HRM include:** Human Resource Planning, Training and Development, Organisational Development, Employee Retirement and Separation, Performance Appraisal, Personnel Research, Career Planning, Compensation, Labour Welfare, Industrial Relations and Record-keeping.

- **Organisation of HRM involves:** It involves: 1. Personnel department in Line Organisation, 2. Personnel department in Functional Organisation and 3. Personnel department in Line and Staff Organisation.

- HRM plays different roles in an organisation such as policy maker, advisor, record-keeper, counsellor, legal consultant, coordinator etc. It gives roadmap for managers for their various issues such as recruitment, selection, promotion etc.

- Human resource manager has to play three kinds of roles i.e. Administrative, Operational and Strategical.

- Various challenges faced by HRM include: Finding the Right Talent, Managing Labour and Benefit Costs, Maintaining Work Culture, Managing Low Attrition Rate and Economical and Technological Changes.

Multiple Choice Questions

1. What is the meaning of the acronym HRM?
   (a) Human Relations Management　　　(b) Humanistic Resource Management
   (c) Human Resource Management　　　(d) Humane Resource Management

2. Which of the following terms was also used before the language of modern HRM? Select all that apply.
   (a) Personnel management   (b) Industrial relations
   (c) Labour relations   (d) Staff management
3. What is meant by the acronym CIPD?
   (a) Chartered Institute of Personnel and Development
   (b) Chartered Institute of Performance Development
   (c) Chartered Institute of Personnel Directors
   (d) Chartered Institute of People and Development
4. What is meant by the acronym SHRM?
   (a) Soft Human Resource Management
   (b) Strategic Human Resource Management
   (c) Superior Human Resource Management
   (d) Sophisticated Human Resource Management
5. The characteristics of human resources are ...... in nature
   (a) homogeneous   (b) heterogeneous
   (c) ductile   (d) none of the above
6. Which of the following is not a function normally performed by the HR department?
   (a) Recruitment and selection   (b) Training and development
   (c) Pay and reward   (d) Employee relations
   (e) Accounting
7. It has been said that some HR departments have had a 'Cinderella' image. What is meant by this statement?
   (a) Low status and obscure   (b) Bureaucratic
   (c) Old fashioned and staid   (d) Influential and powerful
8. The early roots of contemporary HRM can be traced to which period?
   (a) 1940s   (b) 1970s
   (c) 1890s   (d) 1920's
9. Human resource management is normally ...... in nature.
   (a) Proactive   (b) Reactive
   (c) Combative   (d) None of the above
10. The human resource management functions aim at ......
   (a) Ensuring that the human resources possess adequate capital, tool, equipment and material to perform the job successfully
   (b) Helping the organisation deal with its employees in different stages of employment
   (c) Improving an organisation's creditworthiness among financial institutions
   (d) None of the above

Answer to MCQ's

(1) – (c), (2) – (a), (3) – (a), (4) – (b), (5) – (b), (6) – (c), (7) – (a), (8) (c), (9) – (a),
(10) – (a)

Project Questions

1. In your opinion, what is the most important role of an HR manager?
2. Visit any company and observe the functions of Human Resource Management.

Case Study

Companies are on the lookout for young talent to take under their wings. DBS Bank for example, is hoping to expand its banking talent pool by hiring 200 fresh graduates for four newly launched talent development programmes. Aimed at diploma and degree holders who have graduated recently, the programmes will groom talent aspiring to build careers in retail banking, Small and medium sized enterprise (SME) banking and customer service.

While the business recovery remains shaky, pay rises in the region are expected to be steady. The tightening of the labour market in 2014 is expected to push local salaries up, says Goh. "With the new 'Fair Consideration Framework employment guidelines', the focus will be very much on local hires."

Candidates' expectations have also gone up. Quite a number of candidates, from fresh graduates to experienced hires, are looking for higher salaries, says Goh. "Besides the tightening labour situation, wages will also be affected by the economic slowdown, inflation, and company performance."

Hellemons from Adecco concurs. "Salaries are expected to increase. As in 2013, we are seeing organisations compete to attract and retain the very best talent. HR professionals within companies will be looking into competitive compensation packages," she says.

Employees in Singapore can expect an average of a 4.5% salary increase in 2014, which is a positive development after taking into account expected inflation of 2.9% versus 4.6% in 2012, says Sean Paul Darilay, Global Data Services Leader-Southeast Asia, Towers Watson. "This is a welcome development as employees have been feeling significant cost-of-living pressures in the last few years."

Bonuses will still be good for companies that are doing well, but most SMEs and multinationals tend to be more conservative on this payout, especially those international organisations affected by the sluggish US and European economies, says Goh. "Generally, the commercial sector will adopt a wait-and-see approach. Bonuses will be subject to industry productivity and profitability. Most companies will follow the government-recommended guidelines and inflation rate in Singapore."

Provision of health-care benefits remains important, with most companies providing clinical and outpatient cover, as well as hospitalisation benefits, says Darilay. "Consistent with the recent trend towards workforce well-being, we observe a notable increase in the provision of wellness and healthcare programmes. Overall, benefits programmes remain an integral part of a company's attraction and retention strategy."

Questions:

1. Analyse the case and find out the problem area.
2. How does environment affect the HR policies of the company?
3. What HR policies and practices may company follow in future to secure youth's expectation without harming the organisation?

Questions for Discussion

1. Define HRM. Explain the Scope and Importance of HRM.
2. What is HRM? State the Importance of HRM. Explain the Scope and Objectives of HRM.
3. Define Human Resource Management. Explain in Detail Importance and Functions of HRM.
4. Explain Role and Scope of Human Resource Management and Personnel Management in the Overall Success of an Organisation.
5. What is Human Resource Management? Explain Difference between Human Resource Management and Personnel Management.
6. Explain Organisation and Role of HRM Department in a Large Scale Industrial Unit.
7. Define Human Resource Management. Explain Scope and Importance of HRM in an Organisation.
8. Define Human Resource Management (HRM). Differentiate between HRM and Personnel Management.
9. Describe the Function of HRM.
10. Write Short Notes:
    (A) Limitations of HRM.
    (B) Importance of HRM.

✍ ✍ ✍

Chapter **3**...

Procurement

Contents ...

3.1   Human Resource Planning

     3.1.1   Definitions of Human Resource Planning

3.2   Recruitment

3.3   Selection

- Points to Remember
- Questions for Discussion
- Multiple Choice Questions
- Project Questions
- Case Study
- Questions From Previous Pune University Examinations

Learning Objectives ...

- ➤ To examine the nature and importance of Human Resource Planning.
- ➤ To learn about the factors affecting HRP.
- ➤ To understand the employee planning process.
- ➤ To explore the recruitment concept with the sources and methods.
- ➤ To study the selection concept with its procedures.
- ➤ To understand the difference between recruitment and selection.

3.1   HUMAN RESOURCE PLANNING

In the modern times, planning the activities to attain the goals or objectives has become very important in almost all fields such as economics, political, business etc., Planning involves selecting missions, objectives and the actions to achieve them. It requires decision-making i.e., choosing from among the best alternative future courses of an action or actions. Planning provides a rational approach to achieve pre-selected objectives. Planning bridges the gap from where one is to and where that one wants to go. It makes possible for things to take place in the desired manner. Although, it is very difficult to predict the exact future and although factors beyond control may interfere with the best-laid plans, unless we plan, we are leaving events to chance. From this point of view, planning is an intellectually demanding process, it requires consciously determined courses of actions and to base various decisions on purpose, knowledge and considered estimates. Planning is essentially concerned with future and since future conditions are unknown, forecasts or estimates must be made properly to provide a basis for successful planning. In simple words, planning is deciding the course of action to be followed for achieving the objectives.

So far as the business organisations are concerned, in all organisations, plans are prepared for different functions such as purchasing, production, marketing, human resource management, etc. and at various levels of management. However, implementation of the plans depend to a greater extent on the available human resources in an organisation and hence, suitable employees or human resources must be available in the organisation as per the requirements. For making available suitable employees as and when they are needed, 'Human Resource Planning', which is also known as 'Manpower Planning', is required to be carried out. In this chapter, we will to study different aspects relating to Human Resource Planning such as recruitment, selection, etc., Therefore, let us first try to understand the meaning of 'Human Resource Planning' with the help of some definitions stated by the experts in the field of Human Resource Management.

3.1.1 Definitions of Human Resource Planning

Human resource planning means deciding the number and type of human resources required for each job, unit and the company in order to carry out organisational activities. It is a process by which an organisation moves from its current manpower position to its desired manpower position. It is influenced by the strategic management of the company.

Human Resource Planning, also known as 'Manpower Planning', involves identifying staffing needs by analysing properly the available human resources and determining what additions and/or replacements are required in order to maintain the staff of the desired size and quality. It can be at different levels and for different purposes. At the national level, manpower planning is done by the Government for economic development, such as population projections, educational facilities, etc. Such manpower planning is also known as macro-level planning.

Definitions :

1. According to **Lean C. Megginson,** *"Human Resource Planning is an integrated approach to performing the planning aspects of the personnel function in order to have a sufficient supply of adequately developed and motivated people to perform the duties and tasks required to meet organisational objectives and satisfy the individual needs and goals of organisational members."*

2. According to **E.B. Geisler,** *"Manpower planning is the process including forecasting, developing and controlling, by which a firm has the right number of people, at the right places, at the right time; doing work for which they are economically most useful."*

3. According to **Eric W. Vetter,** *"Manpower planning is the process by which management determines how the organisation should move from its current manpower position to its desired manpower position. Through planning, management strives to have right number of and the right kind of people at the right place at the*

right time, doing things which result in both, the organisational and the individual, receiving maximum long run benefits."

4. According to **Coleman,** *"Human Resource or Manpower Planning is "the process of determining manpower requirements and the means for meeting those requirements in order to carry out the integrated plan of the organisation."*

5. According to **Strainer,** *Manpower Planning is "strategy for the acquisition, utilisation, improvement and preservation of an enterprise's human resources. It relates to establishing job specifications or the quantitative requirements of jobs determining the number of personnel required and developing sources of manpower."*

6. According to **Gordon MacBeath,** *"Manpower planning involves two stages. The first stage is concerned with the detailed planning of manpower requirements for all types and levels of employees throughout the period of the plan and the second stage is concerned with Planning of manpower supplies to provide the organisation with the right type of people from all the sources to meet the planned requirements."*

7. According to **James J. Lynch:** *"Manpower planning is "the integration of manpower policies, practices and procedures so as to achieve the right number of the right people at the right jobs at the right time."*

8. **W.S. Wistrom** rightly pointed out in the Conference Board Report, *"Manpower planning Evolving System"*, that manpower planning can be seen as a series of activities consisting of the following:

    (a) Forecasting future manpower requirements, either in terms of mathematical projections of trends in the economic environment and development in industry or in terms of judgement estimates upon the specific future plans of the company.

    (b) Making an inventory of present manpower resources and analysing and assessing the extent to which these resources are employed optimally.

    (c) Anticipating manpower problems by projecting present resources into the future and comparing them with the forecast of requirements to determine their adequacy, both quantitatively and qualitatively.

    (d) Planning the necessary programmes of recruitment, selection, training, development, utilisation, transfer, promotion, motivation and compensation to ensure that future manpower requirements are properly met.

Objectives of HRP:

(a) To establish and to recognise future job requirements.

(b) To assure supplies to qualified human resources.

(c) To develop available human resources.

(d) To utilise the current and prospective human resources.

(e) To decide a sound and suitable recruitment policy.

(f) To introduce effective labour cost reduction measures.

Apart from the above listed objectives, there are many important objectives which are listed below:

1. **Focusing on the Area where Human Resource is Required:** There could be some departments or sections in an organisation where there are less number of employees appointed than required. In such cases present employees get burdened and lose interest in their work. So it is the responsibility of the human resource planning department to see the fulfilment of the requirement of the respective section, to generate efficient performance from the employees.

2. **Making Manpower Available as and when Required:** In sectors like information technology, attrition is the biggest problem. Finding and providing the right person, at the right place and right time is crucial. In such cases the human resource planning department should have a readymade plan for filling that position with the given budget. The human resource planning department has to anticipate the number of employees required in future to avoid delay.

3. **Controlling the Cost of Human Resource:** Making people happy with the same salary in these high inflation times is a tough task for the human resource department. Manpower planning tries to reduce labour costs, recruitment and replacement costs.

4. **Providing Training and Development Programmes:** To compete in the changing technology, an organisation has to take initiative towards the employee development. Analysing the future requirement of the company and finding the skill set required is the basic objective of the organisation. This will make employees ready for the future changes and organisations can save time on finding people from outside.

5. **Coping up with Changes:** HR planning is required to cope up with changes in the market condition, technology, products and government regulations in an effective way.

Merits and Demerits of HRP

Merits :

1. **Improvement of Labour Productivity:**
   - Manpower or human resources as a factor of production differs from other factors of production. As it is subject to its free will, the productivity of labour can be improved if the workers are kept satisfied.
   - In other words, just as satisfied workers can be productive, dissatisfied workers can be destructive.
   - Therefore, through proper human resource planning we can improve the morale of the labour and improve labour productivity.

2. **Recruitment of Qualified Human Resources:**
   - Talented and skilled labour has become a scarce resource especially in developing countries. Therefore, for the long run survival of a firm, it is essential to recruit the best labour force through proper manpower planning.

3. **Adjusting with the Rapid Technological Change:**

   - With the change in technology, the job and job requirements are also changing. Therefore, it is necessary to forecast and meet the changing manpower, which can withstand the challenges of the technological revolution. This can be done only through effective manpower planning.

4. **Reducing Labour Turnover:**

   - The labour turnover refers to the mobility of labour out of the organisation due to various factors such as dissatisfaction, retirement, death etc.
   - Due to labour turnover, a firm will be losing experienced and skilled labour force. This loss can be minimised only through efficient manpower planning.

5. **Control over Recruitment and Training Cost:**

   - Highly skilled personnel are in short supply and it is very costly to hire, train, and maintain them.
   - A company has to incur heavy costs in processing the applications, conducting written tests, interviews etc., and in the process of providing adequate training facilities.
   - In consideration of these costs, it is essential to plan carefully in relation to the manpower so as to reduce the recruitment and training cost.

6. **Mobility of Labour:**

   - Today, it is very difficult to maintain the qualified personnel in an organisation as they will be moving from one job to another in search of better prospects.
   - In a free society, human beings enjoy unrestricted mobility from one part of the country to the other.
   - Therefore, in order to reduce the loss of experienced and skilled labour, every organisation must have a sound system of manpower planning.

7. **It cans Facilitate Expansion Programmes:**

   - In these days of rapid industrial development, every company goes for expansion of its activities.
   - As a result of the increasing company size, the demand for human resources also increases. This necessitates proper manpower planning so as to ensure the continued supply of the required manpower for the firms' activities.

8. **To Treat the Manpower like Real Corporate Assets:**

   - Today it is being increasingly felt by the practising managers and psychologists that men in an organisation must be treated like the most significant assets.
   - The productivity of a company can be improved only through manpower planning, recognizing the significance of the human factor in business.
   - Proper manpower planning considers the fact that satisfied workers can contribute a lot to the overall profitability of the firm through improved productivity.

Demerits of Human Resource Planning

- **Unpredictability:** Although human resource planning has the potential to give your business a greater degree of stability by building the skills of the workforce, there is no guarantee that the workers you train will stay with their company long enough for you to reap the benefits of your investment.

- **Expense:** It costs a company to train and invest in their staff. Whether they are paying for dedicated training or diverting employee hours from tasks that are more likely to directly increase their incoming revenue, human resource planning may likely decrease your bottom line in the short term before it increases your profits in the long term.

- **Illusion of certainty:** While human resource planning can make your workforce better able to do your jobs, you may be training personnel to perform functions that become obsolete as your company and your industry evolve. This can give you a false sense of security and may prevent you from reacting quickly enough to developments.

Process of Human Resource Planning

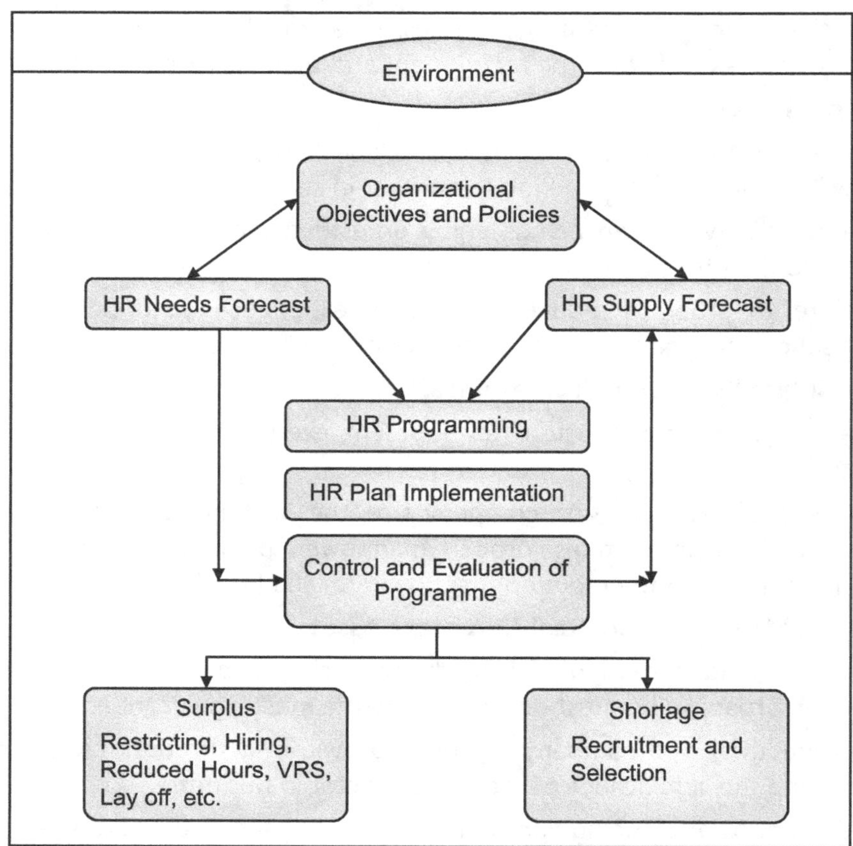

Fig. 3.1: Process of Human Resource Planning

1. **Environmental Scanning:** It monitors those external forces which influences the organisation. Managers monitor economic factors, technological changes, demographic changes, political and legal issues and social concerns. By scanning the environment, organisations can take precautionary action to protect organisations from future losses.

2. **Organisational Objectives and Policies:** Organisational policies are based on objectives. The number and type of employees could be decided as per the objectives of an organisation. After getting a clear understanding of the objectives, the HR department has to handle those concerns which management has for an organisation.

3. **HR Needs Forecast:** An organisation has various demands which need to be fulfilled from time to time. Demands / need forecasting can help in:

   (a) Measuring the job requirements necessary for producing a given number of goods or services.

   (b) Determining the staff mix which is desirable in the future.

   (c) Analysing the exact requirement of the staff for the respective sections or departments so as to reduce costs.

   (d) Maintaining and retaining potential employees for the benefit of an organisation.

   (e) Monitoring compliance with legal requirements with regards to the reservation of the job.

4. **HR Supply Forecast:** Forecasting of manpower supply is essential to meet the future demands. It measures the number of people likely to be available from internal and the external environment.

   Internal Labour Supply: A profile of employees in terms of age, gender, education, training, experience, job level, past performance and future potential should be kept ready for use whenever required. Requirement of growth and transfers should also be assessed in advance.

   Internal sources are important for specific reasons:

   (a)　They carry forward the organisational culture.

   (b)　Internal mobility acts as a motivational factor.

   (c)　Fewer efforts are required on training of personnel.

   (d)　They are well aware of the policies and procedures of the company.

   (e)　Cost on recruitment is reduced.

   External Labour Supply: When the organisation expands rapidly, they need to fulfil the labour requirement from outside. There are various external supply sources like consultants, advertisements, casual applications, candidates referred by current employees, educational institutes etc.

External sources are important for specific reasons:

(a) Young candidates and new experience will be available.

(b) Organisation needs to replace lost personnel.

(c) Organisational growth and diversification creates the need to use external sources to obtain additional number and type of employees.

5. **HR Programming:** The focus of HR programming is to ensure that the vacancies created through demand and supply forecast can be filled by the right persons, at the right places, doing the right job, at the right cost. Thus the existing number of personnel and their skills are compared with the forecasted needs of identified gaps and the HR programme is prepared accordingly.

6. **HR Plan Implementation:** The human resource requirements need to be identified along with the procedure to meet those requirements; this means preparing an HR plan. It should be supported by relevant polices, programmes and strategies.

There are a number of HR strategies:

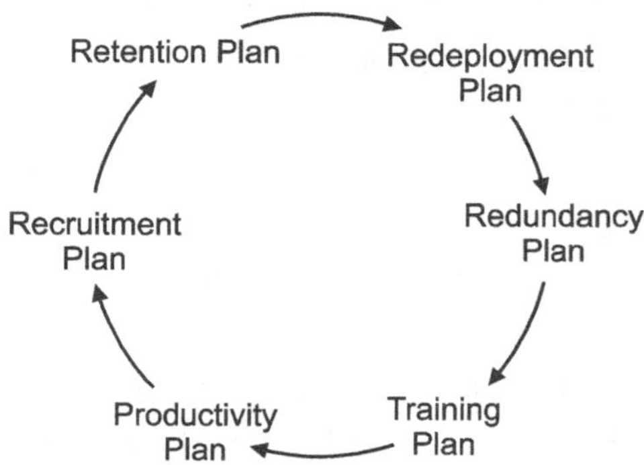

Fig. 3.2: HR Plan Implementation

(a) **Recruitment Plan:** It estimates the number and type of employees needed. Special plans for recruiting the right person, at the right place and the right method for recruiting them is decided.

(b) **Redeployment Plan:** It provides information about transferring or retraining existing employees for a new job.

(c) **Redundancy Plan:** It finds out the areas of redundant jobs or where excess employees are doing the same job. Finding out the redundancy will save the cost of the company by retrenching them systematically.

(d) **Training Plan:** It estimates the number of trainees and apprentices required in the present and future. It also gives an idea about the type of new courses to be developed or changes required in present employees.

(e) **Productivity Plan:** This determines the reasons for employees' productivity and mechanisation for improving productivity.

(f) Retention Plan: It indicates the reasons for employees' turnover and stipulates strategies to avoid wastage through compensation policies, changes in the work requirement and improvement in working conditions.

7. **Control and Evaluation of Programme:** Controlling the activities of human resource needs to be verified through surplus and shortage of employees.

   When there are surplus employees, retrenching of employees is needed which indicates:

   (a) Who is to be redundant, when and where.

   (b) Plans for redevelopment or re-training.

   (c) Steps to be take for helping redundant employees to find new jobs.

   (d) Policies for declaring redundancies and making redundancy payments.

   (e) Programme for dealing with surplus labour by retaining all employees but reducing the working hours.

Factors Influencing on HRP

Fig. 3.3: Factors influencing on Human Resource Planning

1. **Organisational Growth Cycle and Planning:** When an organisation is undergoing a growth stage, forecasting of manpower is essential. A mature organisation experiences less flexibility and variability.

2. **Environmental Uncertainties:** Environmental uncertainty includes social, political and economical changes which affect the organisation. Personnel planners deal with environmental uncertainties by carefully planning, recruiting, selecting, training and developing policies and programmes.

3. **Time Horizon:** In the long-term companies need to plan for their manpower supply. Factors like short-run competitors, rapid changes in social and economical conditions and unstable product or service demands affect organisation. There are also long-run strong competitors, evolutionary changes, and strong management practices that affect an organisation

4. **Outsourcing:** Normally organisations outsource the recruiting part so as to reduce the wastage of time. These are non-critical activities which are subcontracted to a third party. It makes the process of recruiting and interviewing easy for HR. Today many outsourcing firms are providing efficient services to organisations in turn saving huge amounts for them.

5. **Labour Market:** It includes a bunch of people possessing skills and abilities that can be captured, as and when the need arises. India will need 30 million skilled workers by 2015 as per the Confederation of Indian Industry (CII). Labour market affects HRP because the desired skilled manpower may or may not be available. It hampers the growth and productivity of an Industry. Efficiency may also reduce because of employing semi-skilled or unskilled workers.

6. **Type and Quality of Information:** For right forecasting, right information has to be available. One of the major issues in personnel planning is the availability of information which can be used in marketing forecast. An organisation has to segregate the type of information according to the level of application and scope of that information in future. For example: **Strategic Information** includes information on product mix, customer mix, competitive advantage, geographical constraints for expansion etc. **General Information** includes information on organisational structure, information flow, functional areas, supply and distribution channels, sales territories, changing technology etc. and **Specific Information** includes information on job evaluation, skills inventories, management inventories, recruitment sources etc.

Manpower planning plays an important role at both micro as well as macro level. It is found today that more complex technologies are functioning in economic, social, business environments. As a result, the organisations face shortages of the right type of human resources. Manpower planning enables to get the right type of personnel in the organisation. Besides this, following points also throw the light on the importance of manpower planning:

Importance :

(a) Manpower planning involves forecasting of manpower requirements in an organisation and helps the management in-anticipating personnel shortages and surpluses and also to develop the ways to avoid or correct problems before they become serious. Further, forecasting of long-range manpower requirements is helpful in forecasting the compensation costs involved in that connection.

(b) A proper and systematic forecasting of human resource requirements helps an organisation to determine proper sources and methods of recruitment. Further, an organisation can also adopt a proper selection procedure depending upon the needs of the jobs. Proper tests can be designed for the purpose of selecting the right candidates for the right jobs. Thus, importance of manpower planning is immense in recruiting and selecting of the personnel.

(c) From the view point of training and development, the importance of manpower planning is definitely great. Manpower planning ensures training of employees in an organisation. Training involves imparting of knowledge and developing attitudes, skills, social behaviour, etc., of the employees. Manpower planning identifies the training needs of the personnel of an organisation beforehand so that necessary arrangements and training programmes can be chalked out accordingly to give the training to the employees. Training helps the organisation to utilise its human resources to the optimum. Manpower planning is not only important from the view point of an organisation but also helps the employees of an organisation in developing and in the application of skills, abilities, knowledge which affect their capacity positively as for as efficiency, earnings, etc., are concerned.

(d) So far as performance appraisal is concerned, manpower plays an important role in that area too. Performance appraisal refers to identification of strengths and weaknesses of the employees of an organisation relating to their jobs. It is conducted to know whether the existing human resources possess the necessary qualities and qualifications as per the requirements of the jobs. Manpower planning makes available necessary strategies to correct the weaknesses of the employees by making the proper arrangements for corrective training, retraining, orientation programmes. As a matter of fact, all these are inter-related activities.

(e) Importance of manpower planning is none the less in respect of controlling the labour costs. Efforts are made in manpower planning to assure the timely and sufficient supply of labour, thus, avoiding the shortages and surpluses of labour which leads to save and control labour costs.

(f) Manpower planning facilitates career development of employees. Career development refers to development of the career of the personnel employed in an organisation. Taking into consideration the long range plans of the organisation, manpower planning can be done. The plans are made known to the employees who can plan their career accordingly within the organisation. This leads to further development of employees and motivates them. This role of manpower planning is very important.

(g) An organisation develops properly only when there are better results in the form of higher productivity and efficiency. Manpower planning ensures organisational development from this point of view. If manpower planning is done properly and systematically, problems of low productivity, absenteeism, inter-deparmental conflicts, resistance to change, etc., can be tackled and solved efficiently.

Thus, it can be said that manpower planning definitely helps to increase the prospects of an organisation in managing its resources in a better way and coping more effectively with dynamic situations.

Though manpower planning is an important tool in the hands of management and is quite useful, it suffers from certain limitations. These limitations basically arise from the uncertainty of predictions, methods used, etc.

3.2 RECRUITMENT

Concept Of Recruitment : Recruitment is the process of finding and hiring the best-qualified candidate for a job opening, in a timely and cost effective manner, from within or outside of an organisation. The recruitment process includes analysing the requirements of a job, attracting employees to that job, screening and selecting applicants, hiring and integrating the new employee into the organisation.

Definitions of Recruitment:

(a) **Edwin Flippo:** *"Recruitment is the process of searching for prospective employees and stimulating them to apply for jobs in the organisation".*

(b) **Dale Yoder:** *"Recruitment is a process to discover the sources of manpower, to meet the requirements of the staffing schedule and employ effective measures for attracting the manpower in adequate numbers, to facilitate selection of an effective working force".*

(c) **Werther and Keith:** *"Recruitment is the process of finding and attracting capable applicants for employment. The result is a pool of applicants from which new employees are selected".*

(d) **Dale S. Beach:** *"Recruitment is the development and maintenance of adequate manpower resources and it involves the creation of a pool of available labour upon whom the organisation can depend when it needs additional employees".*

(e) **William F. Glueck:** *"Recruitment is that set of activities which an enterprise uses to attract job candidates who have the abilities and attitudes needed to help the enterprise to achieve the objectives".*

(f) **Plumbley:** *"Recruitment is a matching process and the capacities and inclinations of the candidates have to be matched against the demands and rewards inherent in a given job or career pattern".*

From the above mentioned definitions stated by the experts in the field of human resource management, we come to know the following important points so far as the recruitment is concerned.

1. Recruitment is the important process of attracting applicants with certain capabilities, skills, attitudes etc., to job vacancies in an organisation.

2. Recruitment helps to develop and maintain adequate manpower resources.

3. Recruitment helps to create a pool of applicants from which new employees can be selected.

4. Recruitment is a matching process.

5. Recruitment lays foundation for selection of employees.

6. Recruitment is a two-way process. It helps both i.e., a recruiter and a recruitee. A recruiter gets a choice as to whom to recruit from among the pool. While a recruitee also can decide whether he should apply for the job in the organisation considering his abilities, future prospects and his expectations.

There are various objectives or purposes of recruitment. Following are some of the important

Objectives of Recruitment:

1. To attract candidates having the desired qualities and qualifications to meet the organisation's present and future needs.

2. To create a pool of candidates with minimum cost.

3. To fill the vacancies created in the organisation due to promotions, termination, transfers, retirements etc., as well as due to expansion, diversification etc.

4. To help the selection process to become successful.

5. To ensure that the candidates will not leave the organisation atleast in the short period once they are selected.

6. To create and develop organisational and individual effectiveness in short as well as in the long-run and also to develop an organisational culture which may help attract competent people towards the organisation.

7. To help evaluate the effectiveness of various recruitment techniques and sources for various types of job applicants.

Recruitment policy makes the objectives and principles of recruitment clear and also provides a framework for implementation of recruitment programmes and procedures.

Any recruitment policy should comprise the points listed below:

1. Meeting objectives of the company in the given time span i.e. short term and long term.

2. Identifying the need for recruitment.

3. Recruiting staff with the appropriate skills in order to satisfy the needs of the job.

4. Conducting recruitments centrally or de-centrally.

5. Keeping recruitments in line with the company's annual business plan.

6. Filling the positions through Internal or External sources.

7. Specifying the degree of flexibility with regards to skills, qualification and abilities.

8. Determining the criteria of selecting employees.

Sources Of Recruitment :

1.   Internal Sources of Recruitment.

2.   External Sources of Recruitment.

1.   The Internal Sources of Recruitment :

It refer to sources within an organisation and these are the most obvious sources. Whenever vacancies occur, suitable employees already employed in an organisation are promoted, transferred or demoted. Sometimes, retired managers and other employees are also invited to fill the vacancies; especially for a short duration (e.g. leave-vacancies). Promotions and transfers are considered as good sources of recruitment.

Thus, recruitment can be done from the present permanent or temporary employees and retrenched or retired employees. Even the dependents of deceased, disabled, retired and present employees can also be considered for this purpose.

Types of Internal Recruiting:

Internal sources include personnel already on the pay-roll of the organisation. Whenever any vacancy arises, a suitable candidate from within the organisation may be looked at. Organisations consider the candidates from this source for higher level jobs due to availability of most suitable candidates for jobs, to meet the trade union demands and due to the policy of the organisation to motivate the present employees. The internal types of recruitment are as follows:

(a) **Promotion:** Promotion means shifting an employee to a higher position, carrying higher responsibilities, facilities, status and salary. Various positions in an organisation are usually filled up by promotion of existing employees on the basis of merit or seniority or a combination of both.

(b) **Transfer:** Transfer refers to a change in job assignment. It may involve a promotion or demotion or no change in terms of responsibility and status. A transfer may be either temporary or permanent, depending on the necessity of filling jobs. Promotion involves upward mobility while transfer refers to a horizontal mobility of employees.

(c) **Ex-employees:** Ex-employee means persons who have worked in the enterprise and have left the organisation and are eager to return. Such employees with a good record may be preferred. They require less initial training.

(d) **Employee Recommendations:** In order to encourage existing employees, some concerns have made a policy to recruit staff from the applicants introduced and recommended by employees or employees' union. Also preference is given to friends and relatives of existing employees.

Advantages of Internal Sources of Recruitment:

An organisation recruiting employees from internal sources has certain advantages. Some of them are given below:

(a) It is time saving and economical as advertisement for the jobs is not required to be given in external media. Cost of selection is also reduced.

(b) It helps to reduce the executive turnover.

(c) The internal candidates are well versed with policies, rules and regulations of the organisation and as a result, cost of training, induction, orientation, period of adaptability to the organisation etc. can be reduced considerably.

(d) It helps to improve the morale and motivation of employees of the organisation and to develop loyalty towards the organisation and a sense of responsibility.

(e) As the management has better knowledge of the strengths and weaknesses of its employees, proper decisions can be taken to promote or to transfer or to demote and thereby, the chances of making wrong decisions are considerably reduced.

(f) It encourages employees to work hard, sincerely and to put in more effort to get promotions.

Disadvantages of Internal Sources of Recruitment:

Though there are certain advantages of recruitment from internal sources, it also suffers from some disadvantages as mentioned below:

(a) This source of recruitment limits the scope for selection and in addition, there is a possibility of not finding the personnel of required qualities within the organisation.

(b) It prevents the suitable outside candidates with innovative ideas, fresh and constructive thinking and dynamism, from entering the organisation.

(c) If the present employees are promoted or transferred to other posts, their posts get vacant and filling their vacancies may be difficult and then the external sources need to be reached.

(d) There can be bias or some sort of partiality in promoting or transferring the employees from within the organisation which may have adverse effect on the functioning of it. Further, it leads to generation of a feeling of discontent among the employees who are not promoted. Unhealthy competition for promotions or transfers affects morale, performance and motivation of employees adversely.

It should also be noted that excessive dependence on internal sources is dangerous.

Utility of Internal recruitment method in identifying various vacancies

Organisation can save huge amount of expenditure by adopting internal source of recruitment. It boosts morale of an existing employee by giving them promotion options or transfer if they wish so or fit into their policy.

Many organisations rotate job responsibility purposefully so that all employees can get knowledge of an entire organisation also the person who can do best job with what capability or an environment can be identified.

Recruiting ex-employees is also one of the best options in front of an organisation because the persons who has served and know the policies of the company always better than recruiting new entrants. This can saves recruitment, training cost of an organization.

Example 1 : JNPT i.e. Jawaharlal Nehru Port Trust is a central government port follows job rotation of employees so that each employee can understand every task also it boost their confidence by doing different tasks as well. Employees enjoys handling different tasks because of reduction in monotonous work break down

Example 2 : Many private organisations recruit retired people back on their position or on some other position. This can save money on advertisement of those posts and work.

- Utility of External recruitment method in identifying various vacancies.

- To attract new talent, to create positive change, also in order to give a chance to the society new talent external recruitment is a suitable method.

- This can fill vacancies by recruiting people from various agencies, newspaper, recruitment portals etc. This gives wide platform to all people across the globe.

2. External Sources of Recruitment:

The external sources of recruitment refer to all such sources which are outside the purview of an organisation. Important external sources are as mentioned below.

(a) Advertising: Advertising in newspapers and periodicals is one of the most important methods of recruitment, especially for recruitment of management and technical personnel. The company needing manpower advertises details about the job, its requirements, salary, perquisites, duties and responsibilities etc. The advantage of advertising is that all the details about the job can be given in advertisement, to allow self-screening by the prospective candidates. Advertisement gives the management a wider range of candidates to choose from. Its disadvantage is that it brings large number of applications whose screening costs may be quite heavy.

(b) Employment Agencies: There are governments as well as private employment agencies providing a nation-wide or area-wise service in matching personnel demand and supply. In India, there are employment exchanges and bureaus which provide a range of services. In some cases, compulsory notification of vacancies to the employment exchange is required by law. Employment seekers get themselves registered with these exchanges. The employment exchanges bring the job-givers in contact with job-seekers. Employment exchanges are very useful, particularly in the field of unskilled, semi-skilled and skilled operative jobs. However, in the technical and professional areas, private consultancy firms provide recruitment facilities. In big cities, there are several such agencies, prominent among them are: Randstand, Kelly Services, Manpower Consultants, A. F. Ferguson and Company, ABC Consultants etc.

(c) **Gate Hiring:** In a country like ours, where there are a large number of unemployed people, it is usual to find job-seekers thronging the factory gates. Whenever workers are required, people who are present at the gate are recruited in necessary numbers. This method can be used safely for unskilled workers. In some industries, a large number of workers work as *badli* or substitute workers. Whenever a permanent worker is absent, a substitute is employed in his place from among the people present at the gate.

(d) **Educational Institutions:** Direct recruitment from colleges and universities is prevalent for in western countries on a large scale as compared to India. Many big organisations maintain a close liaison with educational institutions for recruitment to various jobs. Various recruiting groups develop systematic university recruiting programmes. They hold preliminary on-campus interviews and select some students for final interview mostly at their offices.

(e) **Labour Unions:** In many organisations, labour unions are regarded as a source to recruit manpower. This facilitates increasing the sense of cooperation and in developing better industrial relations. But sometimes trade unions support a candidate who is not suitable for the job and not acceptable to the management. This weakens the labour relations.

(f) **Field Trips:** An interviewing team makes trips to towns and areas which are known to contain the kinds of employees required by the enterprise. Arrival dates and the time and venue of interview are advertised in advance.

Advantages of External Sources of Recruitment:

(a) It helps to attract and introduce new talent in the organisation which makes the organisation more dynamic through the inflow of innovative ideas, fresh thinking, drive etc.

(b) The best candidates can be selected. It offers wider scope for the selection of employees as there is a possibility that a large number of candidates with the requisite qualities, qualifications and experience may apply for the jobs advertised.

(c) Employees can be selected without pre-conceived ideas, partiality or reservations.

(d) Labour costs can be minimised by selecting the employees on minimum pay scales.

(e) This source proves to be more economical if experienced, well-trained candidates are selected.

Disadvantages of External Sources of Recruitment the company needs to advertise:

(a) It sometimes proves to be expensive, if the company needs to advertise on a large scale and also because of heavy costs of making arrangements for interviews, tests etc.

(b) It is a time consuming and involves a lengthy selection process.

(c) The task of attracting, contacting and evaluating the potential employees is somewhat difficult and strenuous.

(d) It creates unhappiness among the existing employees who feel that they are qualified and fit for the jobs but are not provided with the opportunity. It does not help to develop loyalty among the existing employees.

(e) As newly recruited employees are not familiar with the policies, practices, procedures, environment etc., of the organisation, they take some time to adjust themselves. If they take more time to adjust or if they cannot adjust themselves, valuable time is wasted and costs also increase.

As far as internal and external sources of recruitment are concerned, every organisation has a number of alternative sources for recruitment purposes. However, it should be noted that the best source to tap first is the internal one and then the external. But, in practice, the choice of internal or external source depends to a large extent upon various factors such as: nature of jobs, skills and capabilities required, time available for selection, costs involved, policy and practices of an organisation, situations prevailing in the labour market etc.

Various recruitment sources already studied indicate when and where the human resources can be procured while recruitment methods or techniques throw light on how the various sources are to be tapped. Recruitment methods are in fact the media or means by which an organisation can contact prospective employees and help to provide necessary information, to exchange ideas and also to stimulate the potential employees to apply for the jobs.

Methods of Recruitment: An organisation can use different types of methods to stimulate internal as well as external candidates. Prof. J. D. Dunn and Prof. E. C. Stephens summarised the recruitment methods into three broad categories which are discussed below :

[A] Direct Methods:

Under these methods, job seekers are contacted directly through educational institutions by way of campus interviews. Usually, placement bureaus or offices of the educational institutions provide assistance in attracting job seekers, make arrangements for interviews. Sometimes, recruitees are attracted to attend seminars, conventions at some suitable centres. Some business organisations directly solicit the information with a view to recruit required personnel from the teachers concerned, professors about the students having outstanding records. We generally find campus interviews for M.B.A. students, Engineering students.

[B] Indirect Methods:

Advertisements in publications such as newspapers, trade journals, magazines, technical and professional journals etc., are the important and most frequently used indirect methods of recruitments. We also find advertisements for recruitment on radio, television. Advertisements have proved to be very useful for recruiting blue collar and white collar personnel as well as scientific, technical and professional employees. Of course, the choice of media, timing, place of the advertisements, appeals to job seekers etc., determine the efficiency of advertisements. Advertisement is required to be done in order to be effective and it should give proper and clear-cut idea about the organisation, nature of jobs, job requirements etc.

[C] Third Party Methods:

Private employment agencies, public employment exchanges, employee referrals, trade unions etc., are the mediums through which employees can be recruited. These organisations or institutions are included in the third party methods. In fact, they work as mediators between job seekers i.e., employees and business organisations i.e., employers in order to bring them together. Private agencies charge certain fees for the services they render.

Out of the methods and sources of recruitment mentioned above, a proper method and source is required to be adopted by the organisation. Selection of the best candidate is possible only when maximum number of suitable candidates applies for the post and hence, it is necessary that the method and source of recruitment used should become successful in attracting all such candidates to the organisation. It is also important to decide when the process of recruitment should be started. Depending upon the time required to receive the information from the candidates and the time needed to complete the selection procedure, the recruitment work must begin sufficiently in advance. If the total time required for the recruitment and selection procedure is say, two months and if the post is to be filled at the beginning of September, it becomes clear that the process of recruitment must be started in July.

E-Recruitment: E-Recruitment formally implies sourcing of jobs online (Ganalaki, 2002). E-Recruitment is also known as online recruitment with the help of which the job seekers can send their CV's directly to the employer in an electronic form and their on the other end the employer will receive the CV and can filter is from the other respective candidate's CV's (Finn, 2000). By installing the software like "active recruiting" it is now becoming much easier for the employer to catch the deserving candidate for a particular profile, earlier 62 days were required to fill up vacant position but now it just require 42 days to fill up the same position it is now much easier (willenbrock, 2005). It has been argued that online recruitment cannot replace the traditional way of recruiting but a well implemented online recruitment can help the organization to make their much more easier (caggiano, 1999 & borck, 2000). At the Nike's headquarter they don't miss any of the resume they receive, they treat every CV's to be a prospective one, and the application like "active recruiter" makes it's much easier for them (Nike's, 2005).

Electronic Recruitment has made the job much easier for both the companies and the job seekers and here the credit goes to the Software, IT Professionals, Internet, Computer and many other people who are working back-end. E-Recruitment is an easiest and convincing way to hire people from any part of the world and promotes opportunity, it benefits the company to be recognized globally, E-HRM helps in conveying any kind of HR policies, training program, and pay slip sheets easily. E-HRM is based on more systematic & technology theorem, which helps the HR department to scrutinize employee performance carefully & accurately. It helps in imparting any HR policy; keep a track on employees daily activity report (DAR), efficiently helps the employees in promotion & transfers.

Advantages of E-recruitment :

1. **It's Cost Effective:** "When you post a job ad on Facebook, you can pay for as much or as little exposure as you want, as well as target it to a very specific audience. Indeed, if you manage your campaign effectively, you can save plenty of precious cash, while attracting applicants who are the perfect fit for your vacancy.

2. **It's Immediate :** Most job posts and replies appear in real time. This can help you either increase your efforts to attract more candidates, a different set of candidates (early- instead of mid-career professionals, for example) or even stop candidates from applying if you've already found the right person for the job.

3. **Reduction in the time for recruitment:** The entire cycle of the recruitment get reduced due to online recruitment. From the advertising to selecting, can be done through online at different time and zone. Dependency on physical location will not become a hurdle.

4. **It's Easy :** Almost anyone can post a job advertisement online, because the majority of established job boards make the process clear, easy to understand and user-friendly. Conversely, the process is very simple for the applicant, too, making it quick and painless for interested parties to apply on the spot, as opposed to mailing CVs and written applications through the post.

5. **You Can Make Your Job Ad More Dynamic:** Posting a job online or via social media platforms gives you a chance to be more creative with your ad; for instance, you could create and attach a short video showing off the benefits of working for your company. Indeed, your use of technology can actually say a lot about your company culture, helping to attract specific types of candidates in the process. Businesses that use technology in such a way prove that they aren't afraid to innovate and that they are open to new and interesting ways of doing things.

6. **It's Flexible :** The internet gives you plenty of flexibility with regards to controlling your posts and the applications you receive. If you post in a newspaper and want to amend the job advert, though, you would likely need to pay for an entirely new ad. With online posts, most platforms will allow you to edit, update or remove your job post whenever you wish.

7. **It's Durable:** Newspapers and other forms of printed media have a very limited lifetime, dependent on their publishing cycle. Most classified publications have a biweekly publishing cycle, meaning that your ad will only be seen for that relatively small amount of time. Online job posts, on the other hand, will stay live until the author or the host website removes it.

8. **It's Accessible:** No matter where you are in the world – if you have an Internet-enabled device and connection, then you can perform all those management tasks described above. You can modify your job posting, see how many replies you have and even communicate with candidates directly.

Disadvantages :

1. **Costs Can Spiral:** Depending on the online platform you use, you may have to pay a subscription fee or other costs to post your vacancy. Some sites might even require a membership fee or charge for extra services like application tracking or analytics to manage your advert. Also, if you are not getting the kind of response you're looking for, the costs of leaving the ad to run can accumulate. Screening and checking the skill mapping and authenticity of millions of resumes is a problem and time consuming exercise for organizations.

2. **It Can Be Difficult to Measure Effectiveness:** Not all online recruitment services offer an in-depth analysis of your posting; therefore, it can be hard to figure out what is and isn't working and how to optimise your ad. Of course, this is a common problem in offline recruitment, too, but it's worth remembering that just because you've posted an ad online, it doesn't mean that you will always have access to reams of metrics and supporting data.

3. **It's Informal:** For some roles, companies perceive that online job postings particularly on social media can give off the wrong image of their company. This is particularly true for executive-level roles, particularly at firms (or industries) that have a strong corporate or professional culture.

4. There is low Internet penetration, no access and lack of awareness of internet in many locations across India.

5. Organizations cannot depend solely on the online recruitment methods.

6. In India, the employers and the employees still prefer a face-to-face interaction rather than sending emails.

7. **Huge Competition:** The main downside to following trends is that everybody else is doing the same thing. As a result, your post can quickly become buried under a mountain of other job offers, forcing you to either pay more for extra exposure or risk not being seen. When it comes to social media, you're also at the mercy of Facebook or Twitter's algorithms, meaning that who you target is essentially in the hands of somebody else.

Sr. No.	Traditional Method	Modern Method
1.	It includes trade journals, magazines, professional journals, consultancies, private agencies, public employment exchanges, employee referrals, trade unions etc.	It includes social Networking sites; online job websites, head hunting, poaching, Use of Internet tools and services are the booming ways for the recruitment.
2.	It is more time and cost consuming process.	Modern methods save time of recruiter as well as job seeker.
3.	Newspaper, TV, radios, publications, journals are the traditional recruitment channels.	Fixed low cost hiring, online job portals, e-recruiting, campus recruitment with the internship are the modern recruitment channels.
4.	Company is associated with many consultancies or agencies for their external recruitment.	Employers are associated with online job portal by paying their fees to get CV'S as per mentioned criteria.
5.	Direct, Indirect or third party recruitment involves huge time, money of not only one personnel but a team.	E-Recruitment involves usage of internet tools and services for recruitment of required individuals. It involves skimming through online job portals, job boards like craigslist and getting services of low cost hiring firm to hire candidates.
6.	Unlike poaching employees are retained with the companies' best practices of retention.	Poaching is no more considered as unethical to attract employee by giving them better salary amenities.
7.	Trade journals, magazines, professional journals are used for top levels and executives	Head Hunting for top level managers and executives is a modern approach
8.	Example: Advertisement in Newspapers, radio TV, employment exchange etc.	Example of social networking sites for the recruitment: LinkedIn. Online job seeking websites like Monster.com , Naukri.com

3.3 SELECTION

Concept : Selection is the process of selecting a qualified person who can successfully do a job and deliver valuable contributions to the organisation. It is a system which depends on job analysis. This ensures that the selection criteria are job related.

The requirements for a selection system are knowledge, skills, abilities and other characteristics, known as KSAOs. Personnel selection systems employ evidence-based practices, to determine the most qualified candidates and involve both the newly hired and those who can be promoted from within the organisation.

Two major factors that determine the quality of newly hired employees are: predict or cut-off and selection ratio.

(i) Predict or Cut-off: The predict or cut-off is a test score differentiating those passing a selection measure from those who do not. People above this score are hired or are further considered while those below it are not.

(ii) Selection Ratio: It is a ratio that indicates the selectivity of an organisation from a range of 0 to 1. The selection ratio (SR) is, the number of job openings (n) divided by the number of job applicants (N). This value will range between 0 and 1, reflecting the selectivity of the organisation's hiring practices. When the SR is equal to 1 or greater, the use of any selection device has little meaning. But this is not often the case as there are usually more applicants than job openings. Finally, the base rate is defined by the percentage of employees thought to be performing their jobs satisfactorily following measurement. After using these tools a person is selected for the job.

Definition : Selection is the process of picking or choosing the right candidate, who is most suitable for a vacant job position in an organization. In others words, selection can also be explained as the process of interviewing the candidates and evaluating their qualities, which are required for a specific job and then choosing the suitable candidate for the position.

The selection of a right applicant for a vacant position will be an asset to the organization, which will be helping the organization in reaching its objectives.

Different authors define Selection in different ways:

- Employee selection is a process of putting a right applicant on a right job.
- Selection of an employee is a process of choosing the applicants, who have the qualifications to fill the vacant job in an organization.
- Selection is a process of identifying and hiring the applicants for filling the vacancies in an organization.
- Employee selection is a process of matching organization's requirements with the skills and qualifications of individuals.
- A good selection process will ensure that the organization gets the right set of employees with the right attitude.

Importance of Selection:

Selection is an important process because hiring good resources can help increase the overall performance of the organization. In contrast, if there is bad hire with a bad selection process, then the work will be affected and the cost incurred for replacing that bad resource will be high.

The purpose of selection is to choose the most suitable candidate, who can meet the requirements of the jobs in an organization, who will be a successful applicant. For meeting the goals of the organization, it is important to evaluate various attributes of each candidate such as their qualifications, skills, experiences, overall attitude, etc. In this process, the most suitable candidate is picked after the elimination of the candidates, who are not suitable for the vacant job.

The organization has to follow a proper selection process or procedure, as a huge amount of money is spent for hiring a right candidate for a position. If a selection is wrong, then the cost incurred in induction and training the wrong candidate will be a huge loss to the employer in terms of money, effort, and also time. Hence, selection is very important and the process should be perfect for the betterment of the organization.

Advantages of Selection:

A good selection process offers the following advantages:

- It is cost-effective and reduces a lot of time and effort.
- It helps avoid any biasing while recruiting the right candidate.
- It helps eliminate the candidates who are lacking in knowledge, ability, and proficiency.
- It provides a guideline to evaluate the candidates further through strict verification and reference-checking.
- It helps in comparing the different candidates in terms of their capabilities, knowledge, skills, experience, work attitude, etc.

1. **To meet Equal Employment Opportunity (EEO) Requirements:** This gives equal employment opportunities to all aspirants for that job. Job descriptions need to be written in a manner that is non-discriminatory with regard to age, race, gender, national origin and religious beliefs.

2. **To Maintain Corporate Image and Success:** Some companies may choose employees based on the necessary knowledge, skills and abilities, to perform the job at a minimal of acceptable performance. Employees who perform at a higher level of competence may be considered most valuable performers and are rewarded accordingly. Since above-average employees may be instrumental in driving success, the company may initiate a rather comprehensive hiring process. This process may include several interviews, background checks, skills testing, health check-up, drug testing and reference checks. The company image is at stake while attracting top applicants. Therefore, receptionist, interviewers and company executives strive to make a good impression.

3. **For Employee Security:** Every employee has a basic right to work in a safe environment. Therefore, some companies have clearly defined policies regarding safety, health and security in the workplace. The selection process should include the conscience of the company and every person hired needs to be carefully screened for it. Some companies have third-party vendors that perform criminal background

checks. Required drug tests can identify any potential drug abuse issues prior to employment.

4. **For Employee Retention:** Companies with a well designed employee selection process, understand the importance of retaining these valuable assets. The selection process should be the continuous improvement plan with development programmes like leadership, problem solving and employee rewards programmes like outstanding performance, bonus plans, recognition functions and succession planning.

5. **For Reducing Employee Turnover:** Proper selection will reduce employee turnover. A proper candidate will immediately get adjusted with the environment and would not want to leave the organisation in the short term.

6. **Ensures Proper Utilisation:** Proper selection facilitates optimum use of physical and human resources. A proper candidate ensures the proper utilisation of other resources.

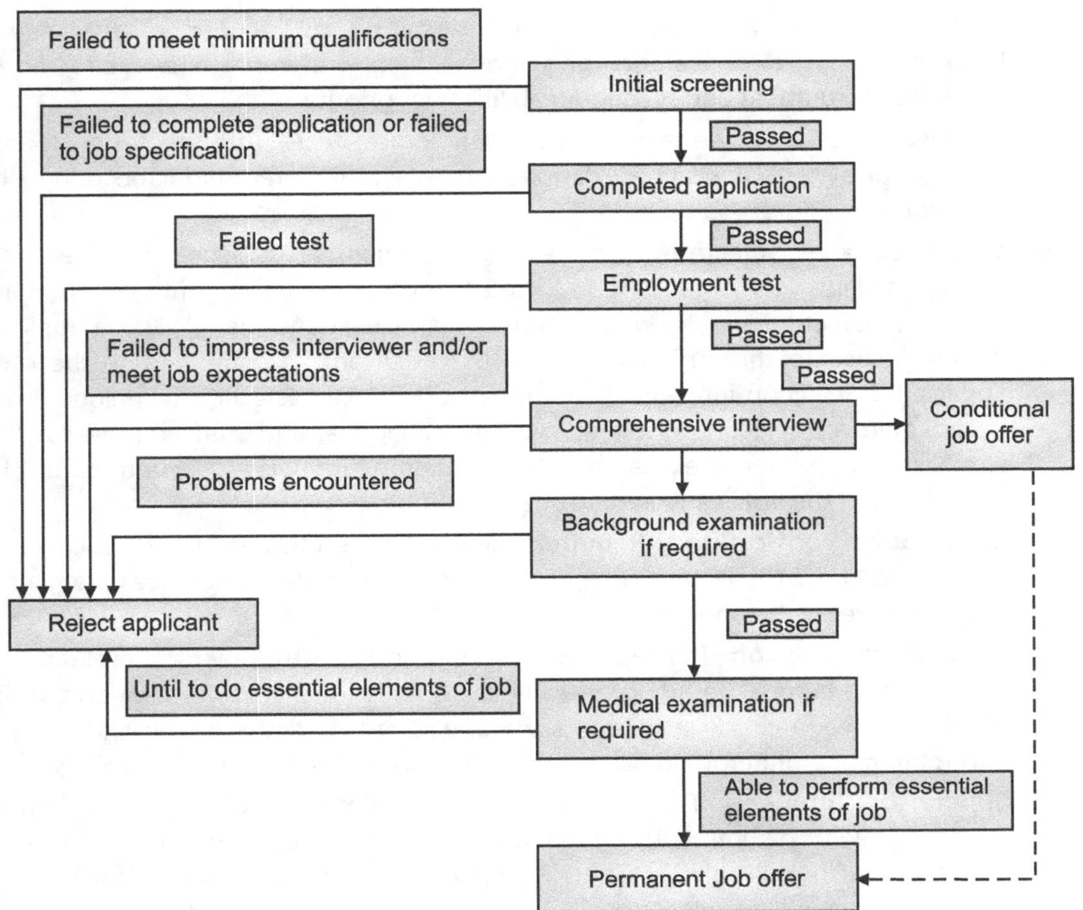

Fig. 3.4: The Selection Procedure

Every organisation has a different method of selection due to its nature, size and style of operation. It also differs according to the posts to be filled in.

The selection process includes the following steps.

(i)   Initial Screening: The first step in the selection process is the screening process. Many candidates get dropped during the initial screening. This step makes the filtration process of candidates easier.

(ii) Completed Application: Blank application forms are provided for getting detailed information about the applicant. The application should typically contain biographical data, educational qualifications, work experience, extracurricular activities, special awards, praise received or other important information etc.

There are some mandatory fields which an applicant cannot keep blank. The officer should check all the details before accepting the application.

(iii) Employment Tests: Companies have different types of tests according to the level and nature of candidates required.

Employment tests vary from job to job. For example, for recruitment of Marketing Executives, physical appearance or smartness gets preference whereas for an HR executive recruitment and managing abilities get priority.

Knowledge tests, Performance tests, Psychological tests, Attitude tests, Honesty tests, Medical tests are some examples of tests which are conducted during the selection procedure.

(iv) Comprehensive Selection Interview: Comprehensive selection interview is a formal, in-depth conversation conducted to evaluate an applicant's acceptability. The management seeks answers to some basic questions like - Will the applicant do the justice to the job? and How is the applicant as compared to the other applicants? Selection interview is the most widely used selection technique. It can be adapted for selecting unskilled, skilled, managerial and staff employees. They also allow a two-way exchange of information. Interviewers learn about the applicant and the applicant learns about the employer.

(v)   Background Verification if Required: All sorts of certificates of the applicant are to be checked by the HR manager at this stage. At least two references are needed in order to verify the applicant.

(vi) Medical Examination: The selection process also includes a medical evaluation of the applicant before the hiring decision is made. Normally, the evaluation consists of filling a health checklist that asks the applicant to indicate health and accident information and undergoing various medical tests at the prescribed hospitals.

(vii) Supervisory Interview: The ultimate responsibility of the success of a newly hired worker lies with his immediate supervisor. The supervisor is able to evaluate the applicant's technical abilities. The HR department provides a supervisor with the best pre-screened applicants available and the supervisor decides whom to hire from those.

(viii) The Final Hiring Decision: Regardless of whether the supervisor or the HR department makes the final hiring decision, hiring actually ends the selection process, assuming that the candidate accepts the job offer. To maintain good public relations the company should notify applicants who are not selected.

Interviews :

Definition: An interview is an answer to know and ascertain how to fit a man to the required job. An interview is beneficial to both the candidate and the organization, for it helps them to grow.

When you split the word 'interview' you get two words, 'inter' and 'view'. This roughly translates to 'between view' or seeing each other. This means that both the groups involved in an interview get to know about one another.

An interview definition can be crafted as a gentle conversation between two people or more where questions are asked to a person to get the required responses or answers.

Types of Interview:

Based on the count of people involved:

1. One-to-one interview (Personal interview):

It is the most common among the interview types, it involves the interviewer asking questions maybe both technical and general to the interviewee to investigate how fit the candidate is for the job.

Example: Posts in small organizations and mid-level and high-level jobs in big organizations.

2. Group interview:

This involves multiple candidates and they are given a topic for discussion. They are assessed on their conversational ability and how satisfactorily they are able to have their own views and make others believe in them. Here, the best among the lot gets selected.

Example: Fresher posts and mid-level sales posts.

3. Panel interview (Committee Interview):

The interviewers here are a group from among the company people who are in a senior position and usually, the panel interview is when the candidate is supposed to make a presentation. But many-a-times it could be for the job interview as well.

Example: Mid-level and high-level jobs.

Based on the Planning Involved:

1. Structured interview (Formal interview or guided interview):

Here in the traditional form of an interview, the questions asked are all in a standard format and the same is used for all the candidates. This is to assess the ability of all the candidates impartially.

Example: Entry-level jobs for fresher.

2. Unstructured interview (Informal interview or conversational interview):

This is the opposite of a structured interview. Here the interviewer has a definite idea in mind about the questions to be asked, but it doesn't follow a certain format. The interviewer may deviate and a conversation type interview follows.

Example: Mid-level job interview for managerial position.

Based on Judging the Abilities:

1. Behavioural-based interview:

The interviewee is asked questions about past work experiences and how it was dealt within a particular situation. This helps the interviewer understand the candidate's future performance based on his past experiences.

Here the candidates need to provide examples when they have handled situations. The probing maybe in detail to assess the candidate's behaviour and responses and this determines the candidate's future job prospects.

Example: Interview for managerial positions, executive posts.

2. Problem-solving interview (Task-Oriented interview):

Here the interviewer is more concerned about problem-solving abilities be it technical, managerial, creative or analytical skills. This is the most common among the interview patterns and it may involve either writing and answering a questionnaire set or answering the technical questions orally.

Example: Interviews for Software recruitments, technical industries, and managerial positions.

3. Depth interview (In-depth interview):

When you need to ascertain everything about the interviewee right from life history, academic qualifications, work experiences, hobbies, and interests; you conduct the depth interview.

Here the interviewer has a clear idea about the questions he will be asking but once the question is asked, he allows the conversation to flow and is more of a listener. This interview takes time and more of a friendly approach of the interviewer towards the interviewee.

Example: For executive posts.

4. Stress interview:

Very rare, but such interviews are conducted to see how the candidate will be able to react in stressful situations and to assess if he will be able to handle the crisis at his job.

Tactics involved include:

- Completely ignore the candidate by maybe, making a phone call in the middle of the interview.

- Or some other tactic like continuously interrupting the candidate when he answers the questions.
- Trying to enforce your point of view forcefully even if he disagrees.
- Asking a whole lot of questions all at once.
- Interrupting him by asking another question not related to his answer.

Example: For banker jobs.

Based on the Facilities or Settings:

1. Telephonic interview:

This interview is conducted over the phone and its main objective is to narrow down the probable list of candidates so that only the most eligible ones finally get shortlisted. This is done in the initial stages and before the personal interview.

Also when the candidate is far-off, the company first conducts a telephonic interview and if satisfied then arranges the travel expenses for a one-to-one interview.

Example: Interview for entry-level jobs.

2. Online interview (Video interview or Skype interview):

This interview may be was done by instant messaging, online chats, email or through videos. This involves the interviewer asking questions just like in a personal interview.

This is done based on situations like if the interviewee resides far-off or if the interview at the appointed time gets cancelled due to valid reasons. Also, it is more convenient for the interviewer that he can fix the interview at his spare time and convey the message to the candidate a few hours before or so.

This helps as the interviewer doesn't need to inform the candidate many days in advance.

Example: Interview for mid-level posts.

3. Job Fair Interview (Career Fair interview):

Here the interviewer does a mini-interview to know the qualifications and the technical knowledge. Then basic technical questions are asked to know if the candidate can proceed further for the main interview. This is a very short interview to net only the potential candidates.

Example: Interviews for fresher jobs held at the college campus.

4. Lunch interview:

This interview is more of a conversational interview mainly designed so that the interviewer gets to know more about the candidate. This also helps the interviewer to assess how the candidate conducts himself in a less-formal environment and how he presents himself.

Example: Interview for managerial and sales posts.

5. Tea interview:

This is the same as a lunch interview but only that it differs in the time limit. Here the interviewee gets less time to prove himself. The interviewer here has a structured format for questioning since there is a time limit.

Example: Interview for positions in the fashion and glamour industry and sales posts.

Based on the Task:

1. Apprenticeship Interview:

Here the candidate is a novice and the interview is a very formal one with general questions and some skill related questions being asked.

Example: Interview for training programmes in organizations.

2. Evaluation interview:

In this interview, a fixed set of questions are asked and a scoring system evaluates the points scored. This type of interview negates the scope of the personal bias of the interviewer.

Example: Interview in corporate organizations

3. Promotion interview:

This is for an employee of the company seeking a higher position for career enhancement purposes.

Example: Interviews in mid-level posts.

4. Counselling interview:

When employees are called and their problems and solutions are discussed within the organization, such meeting type interviews are called counselling interviews.

Example: Interviews in big organizations

5. Disciplinary interview:

Here an individual or number of employees or sometimes the employee union is interviewed for their misconduct or non-performance. This is more sort of a meeting between the manager and the employees to get the problem resolved.

Example: Interviews in big companies.

6. Persuasive interview:

The interviewee here has to persuade the interviewer to accept his point of view as in case of an employee persuading his manager to implement some changes in the policy or a sales manager persisting on selling a product.

Example: Interviews in mid-level managerial posts frequently asked interview questions from the candidate at each step and how to answer them,

Q.1. *Can you tell me a little about yourself?*

Q.2. *How did you hear about the position?*

Q.3. *What do you know about the company?*

Q.4. *Why do you want this job?*

Q.5. *Why should we hire you?*

Q.6. *What are your greatest professional strengths?*

Q.7. *What do you consider to be your weaknesses?*

Q.8. *What is your greatest professional achievement?*

Q.9. *Tell me about a challenge or conflict you've faced at work, and how you dealt with it.*

Q.10. *Where do you see yourself in five years?*

Q.11. *What's your dream job?*

Q.12. *What other companies are you interviewing with?*

Q.13. *Why are you leaving your current job?*

Q.14. *Why were you fired?*

Q.15. *What are you looking for in a new position?*

Q.16. *What type of work environment do you prefer?*

Q.17. *What's your management style?*

E- selection :

A sophisticated web-based application which would be executed on the data collected from the applicants or a kind of electronic interaction among employer and potential candidates so-called e-interview that could be vocal or video-based through which try to find the most appropriate job seeker to take the vacancy is e-Selection

There are two different orientations on company's website:

1. **Recruiting-oriented:** It means the website only publish information about the vacant positions for perspective applicants and

2. **Screening-oriented:** It means the website would collect information from applicants to be used for selection process also company's may use both- (Cappelli, 2001).

   So e-selection could be considered only when there is a set of collected data from applicants which requires screening-oriented for company's website.

E-selection processes are usually difficult but generally e-selection would start when the analysis on data or candidate would start somehow to feed decision-making process. Nevertheless, for example in the multiple purposes e-recruitment process to increase efficiency which Marić and Ilić (2012) introduce so that it consists of :

(a) Attract candidates

(b) Communicate with candidates

(c) Assess candidate

(d) Provide feedback to candidates,

based on the previous definition proposed the selection would start on second step since the knowledge about the applicant would start to form whereas they call it as a pre-selection process during e-recruitment. Chapman and Webster (2003) divide various stages of recruitment and selection as (a) advertising positions, (b) receiving applications, (c) initial screening, (d) and final selection.

Selection starts on third stage whereas according to the second one, initial screening is a pre-selection process. As a result generally we can say e-selection process is composed by two steps as pre-selection and the final selection which would be elaborated more by focusing on different methods of e-selection.

Points to Remember

- **Human resource planning** refers to the estimation of the number and type of people needed during the given period. It is very significant as it helps to understand the future need for HR.

- Human resource planning process is the important phase which includes Environmental Scanning, Defining organisational objectives and policies, HR needs forecast, HR supply forecast, HR programming, HRP implementation and Control and evaluation programme.

- HRP has influencing factors like Organisational growth cycle and planning, Environmental uncertainties, Time horizon, Outsourcing, Labour market and Type and Quality of information.

- **Recruitment** is the process of searching for prospective employees and stimulating them to apply for jobs in the organisation.

- There are two types of sources available for recruitment viz. internal and external.

- The **internal sources** of recruitment refer to sources within an organisation and these are the most obvious sources.

- The **external sources** of recruitment refer to all such sources which are outside the purview of an organisation.

- **Selection** is the process of selecting a qualified person who can successfully do a job and deliver valuable contributions to the organisation.
- **Selection procedure involves:** Initial Screening, Completing Application, Employment Tests, Comprehensive Selection Interview, Background Verification, Medical Examination, Supervisory Interview and the Final Hiring Decision.
- **The selection test should be:** Reliable, Valid, Designed and administered by Qualified People, Well prepared, Suitable, Useful and Standard.
- Selection is different than recruitment. It follows recruitment and required more time than the recruitment.

Questions for Discussion

1. What is Human Resource Planning?
2. Explain the factors influencing estimation of Human Resources.
3. Explain the objectives of Human Resource Planning.
4. Explain the process of Human Resource Planning.
5. Explain the process of selection along with the diagram.
6. What are the sources of recruitment? Define the factors affecting recruitment.
7. Distinguish between recruitment and selection.

Multiple Choice Questions

1. HRP includes ......
   - (a) HR needs forecast
   - (b) HR Supply forecast
   - (c) HR programming
   - (d) All of these
2. Which is the factor affecting HRP?
   - (a) Time Horizon
   - (b) Outsourcing
   - (c) Labour market
   - (d) All of these
3. Recruitment is a ...... process as compared to selection.
   - (a) Long
   - (b) Short
   - (c) Lengthy
   - (d) Very easy
4. Employee referral is an ...... recruitment method.
   - (a) Internal
   - (b) External
   - (c) Both
   - (d) None of these
5. Most common constraints on recruiting include all but ......
   - (a) Image of a firm
   - (b) Budgetary Support
   - (c) Interviewing
   - (d) Organisational Policies
   - (e) Government Policies

6. Ultimately, selection decisions are based on ......

 (a) Personal whims and fancies   (b) Performance

 (c) Turnover potential   (d) Human resource plans

 (e) Nepotism

7. Interview gives the recruiter an opportunity to ......

 (a) Make judgment about the interviewee's enthusiasm and intelligence

 (b) Make him do more struggle to get the job

 (c) To demonstrate how tough the selection process is

 (d) To easily filter out candidates by asking tough questions

8. Interviewing mistake includes all but ......

 (a) Halo Effect

 (b) Personal bias

 (c) Leniency

 (d) Realising that foreign national may have different customs

 (e) Talking too much

9. The first factor in deciding the supply of labour is ......

 (a) Developing staffing tables

 (b) Issuing advertisements

 (c) Preparing replacement charts

 (d) Analysing labour markets

 (e) Auditing present employees

10. The basis for human resource planning is ......

 (a) The economic trends

 (b) Demand for employees

 (c) Strategic plans of the firm

 (d) Budgets

 (e) Supply of employees

Answer to MCQ's

(1) – (d), (2) – (d), (3) – (b), (4) – (a), (5) – (c), (6) – (b), (7) – (a), (8) – (d),
(9) – (e), (10) – (c)

Project Questions

1. Find out the recruitment and selection procedure of any company.

2. Analyse the recent problems of recruitment.

Case Study on Recruitment Policy

Susan Kellerman, the vice-president of marketing for Recharge Manufacturing, made the following announcement at the weekly director's meeting: 'I have good news. 'We can get the large contract with Africot Corporation, All we have to do is complete the project in one year instead of two. I told them, we could do it.'

Mpho Moloi, vice president of human resources, brought Susan bock to reality by reminding her, 'Remember the strategic plan we were involved in developing and we all agreed to? Our present workers do not have the skills and knowledge that are needed to produce the quality that Africot's specific needs require. Under the two-year project timetable, we planned to retrain our present workers gradually. With this new time schedule, we will have to go into the job market and attract new workers who are already experienced in this process. This will cost the company a lot of money if we try and complete the project in one year instead of two. We all need to study and discuss your suggestion further. Sure, Susan, we can do it, but with these limitations, will the project be cost-effective?'

Questions:

1. Do you agree with Mpho Moloi or with Susan Kellerman? Give reasons for your answer.

2. What are the purposes of UR planning?

3. Mpho was involved in the strategic planning of the company. Did this involvement help him to challenge Susan's good news forecast? Discuss.

4. Mpho is not sure they can do the project in one year because of the limitations. He questions the cost-effectiveness of the project. What does this mean?

Questions for Discussion

1. Define HRP. Explain in Detail Process of HRP.

2. State and Explain Various Sources of Recruitment.

3. Define Concept of 'Recruitment'. Explain Sources of Recruitment.

4. Explain various Methods of Recruitment.

5. What is HRP? Discuss its Objectives and Importance.

6. What are the Steps generally followed in a Selection Procedure?

7. Write Short Notes:

    (A) Human Resource Planning.

    (B) Difference between Recruitment and Selection.

✍ ✍ ✍

Chapter **4**...

Training and Development

Contents ...

4.1   Training and Development
- Points to Remember
- Questions for Discussion
- Multiple Choice Questions
- Project Questions
- Case Study
- Questions From Previous Pune University Examinations

Learning Objectives ...

- ➢ To be aware of the meaning, definition, importance and objectives of training.
- ➢ To examine methods of training and evaluation.
- ➢ To understand the concept, nature, process and methods of management development.
- ➢ To study the distinction between training and development.

4.1   TRAINING AND DEVELOPMENT

Training plays an important role in improving an organisation's effectiveness in areas such as productivity, health and safety at work and personal development. Every organisation needs to employ people, train and develop them. Most organisations are aware of this requirement and invest efforts and other resources in training and development. Such investment can take the form of employing specialist training and development staff. It is an investment made for future benefits of an organisation. It provides appropriate outline to the overall capabilities of an employee which helps an organisation to accomplish its goal as well the personal goals of employees. It also helps to change the attitude of employees in order to get better cooperation from their subordinates.

Training is necessary to prepare existing employees to achieve more in their jobs. It is an activity of succession planning of an organisation. It also bridges the gap between requirements of the job and employee's understanding towards that job. Hence it makes a person more productive.

Many companies have adopted this broader perspective, which is known as high-leverage training. **High-leverage training** is linked to strategic business goals and objectives which uses an instructional design process to ensure that training is effective and compares or benchmarks the company's training programmes against training programmes in other companies.

High-leverage training practices also help to create working conditions that encourage continuous learning. **Continuous learning** requires employees to understand the entire work system, including the relationships among their jobs, their work units and the company. Employees are expected to acquire new skills and knowledge, apply them on the job and share the information with their colleagues.

Definitions of 'Training':

- According to **Elmer H. Burack and Robert D. Smith**, *"Training is a planned, organised and controlled activity designed to express some aspect of present job performance. Training is skill-oriented and is usually intended for the short run welfare of the company. Training is also a key ingredient in the motivation of individuals. An untrained, unskilled employee feels very insecure, lacking the self-confidence necessary for comfortable group relations".*

- According to **Prof. Milkovich and Prof. Boudreau,** *"Training is a systematic process of changing the behaviour, knowledge, and / or motivation of present employees to improve the match between employee characteristics and employment requirements".*

- According to **Prof. Arun Monappa and Prof. Mirza Saiyadain**, *"Training refers to the teaching and learning activities carried on for the primary purpose of helping members of an organisation to acquire and apply the knowledge, skills, abilities and attitudes needed by the organisation".* They further opined that *"broadly speaking, training is the act of increasing the knowledge and skill of an employee for doing a particular job".*

Objectives of Training:

1. To Perform the Task: Every task needs certain expertise. An organisation expects tasks to be completed with the given specifications only. To perform those special tasks every personnel should have thorough knowledge about their operating method, for which a company may arrange small workshops or training programmes where an employee gets hands on experience and will have a clear idea about how the task can be preformed.

2. To Bring Effectiveness: After getting knowledge of a particular task, it has to be performed with effectiveness. Training gives accurate information and also some exposure to bring in effectiveness in their work.

3. To Bridge the Gap: Education teaches theory but the training gives practical knowledge about the work. So it bridges the gap between learning a particular thing and actually doing it.

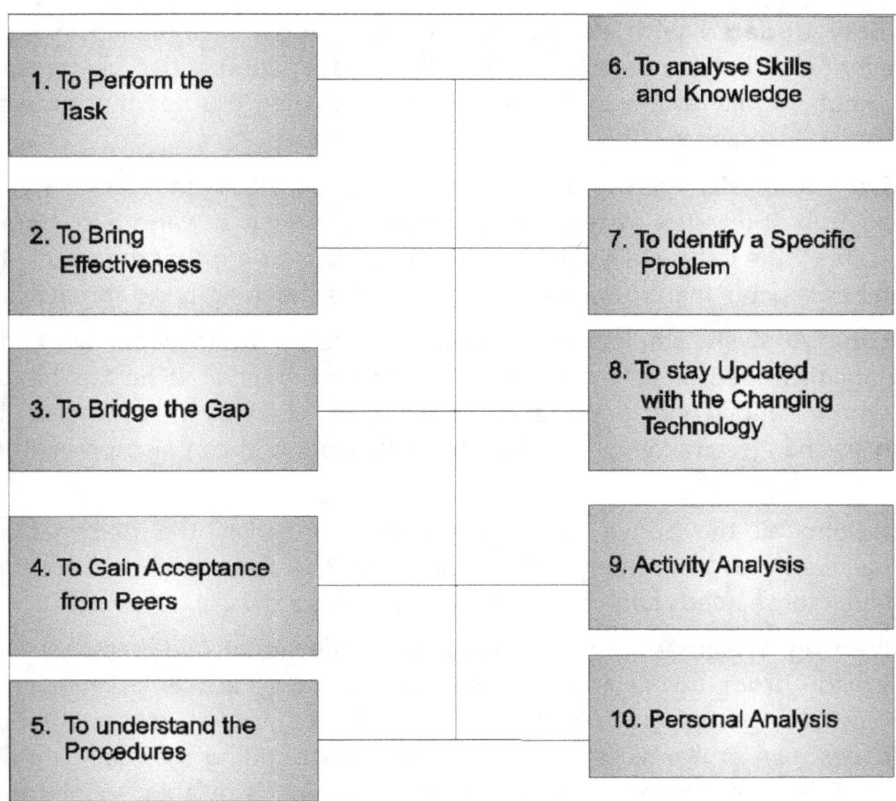

Fig. 4.1: Objectives of Training

4. To Gain Acceptance from Peer Members: Competent people are always accepted well. To gain such acceptance, a person should possess knowledge, experience and judgement. Judgement comes automatically along with experience. But skills and knowledge can be developed through behavioural training programmes.

6. To Understand the Procedure: Misunderstanding often puts a person and an organisation in the situation of losing money and relations with others. To gain correct understanding about the system, a newly appointed person will need to undergo an induction programme so that he can understand the working procedure.

7. To Analyse Skills and Knowledge: Training helps in analysing the specific skills and knowledge which people should posses. Training should be provided to the person lacking the mentioned skill set to focus on the lacking area.

8. To Identify a Specific Problem: Identifying the problem areas related to a person's work is a difficult task. He is unable to give his best due to such unidentified problems. Through training unidentified problems can be definitely found and solved.

Example: A newly appointed person doesn't have adequate knowledge about the machinery or the technology he is working on, due to which he is performing badly. He needs hands-on experience to get acquainted with the new system. Through training he can gain appropriate experience of working on that machine.

9. To Stay Updated with the Changing Technology: Maintaining speed with the changing technology has become essential in the present competitive business world. But everyone cannot be fully aware of new technology. Training ensures that employees stay updated with the changing technology.

10. Activity Analysis: Identifying training needs, activities and tasks are important aspects of any job. It involves systematic and detailed analysis of various components of a job and indicates if the nature of the job has changed over a period of time and whether the organisation has capable manpower who can handle the changing tasks and activities.

11. Personal Analysis: Employees' psychology, attitude towards work, work-life balance and overall abilities need to be reviewed at regular time interval. It reveals his perception about the organisation and importance of work in his life. This analysis helps the organisation to change employees' attitude towards work and can also prevent losses due to wrong perception.

Accomplishing all the above mentioned objectives satisfy the personal as well as organisational needs of any enterprise or company. The follow up and continuation of training will fulfil these needs and make the organisation successful.

1. Converting Weaknesses into Strengths: Professional and personal weaknesses hinders a person from giving the best services. Training assists in eliminating these weaknesses, by strengthening workers' skills. A well organised development programme helps employees gain similar skills and knowledge, thus bringing them all to a higher and uniform level. This simply means that the whole workforce is reliable, so the organisation doesn't have to rely only on a few employees.

2. Performance Improvement: A properly trained employee becomes more informed about procedures for conducting various tasks. The worker's confidence is also boosted by training and development. This confidence comes from the fact that the employee is fully aware of his / her roles and responsibilities. It helps the worker carry out the duties in a better way and even find new ideas to incorporate in the daily execution of duty.

3. Consistency in the Performance: Consistency is vital when it comes to an organisation's procedures and policies. This mostly includes administrative procedures and ethics during execution of duty. Through knowledgeable training programmes, workers can bring in tremendous change in their work which will also bring consistency due to positive impact on overall results.

4. Job Satisfaction: Training and development makes employees feel satisfied with the role they play in the organisation. This is driven by the greater ability they gain to execute their duties. They get a sense of belongingness for the organisation they work for and try to give their best in return.

5. Increases Productivity: Through training and development, the employee acquires all the knowledge and skills needed for his day to day tasks. Workers can complete their tasks at a faster rate and with efficiency thus increasing overall productivity of the company. Employees also learn new tactics of overcoming challenges they face.

6. **Enhances Quality of Products and Services:** Employees learn standard methods to use in their tasks. They are also able to maintain uniformity in the output they give. This helps the company in providing satisfying services or goods.

7. **Minimal Wastage:** Wrong use of machinery leads to wastage of resources and it can also cause accidents at times. Training results in optimal utilisation of resources of an organisation and reduction in accidents. All the machines and resources are used economically, reducing expenditure.

8. **Reduction in Supervision:** Employees become more confident when they gain the necessary skills and knowledge. They become self reliant and require little guidance when they perform their tasks. The supervisor can depend on the employee's decision for quality output. This relieves supervisors from the burden of constantly giving directives on what should be done.

Methods of Training:

Once the organization realises the need for training, the manager needs to design the training programme and the training material. Some training needs actual machinery to practice whereas some trainings are intellectual lectures. Thus training can be given through ON-the-JOB, OFF-the-JOB and WEB based Training.

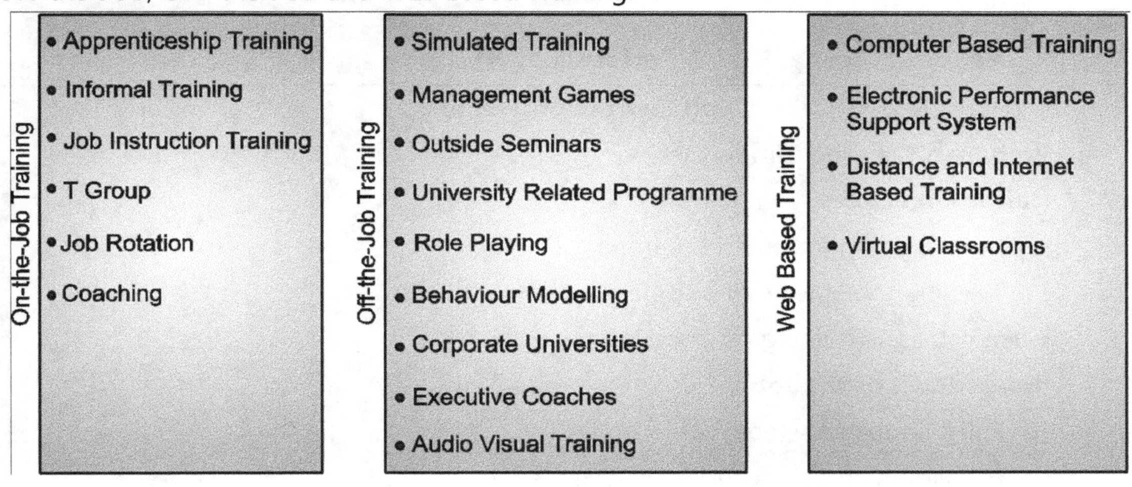

Fig. 4.2

On-the-Job Training: In most firms, this is the only method applied for training. It includes Orientation, Job instruction, Internship, Apprenticeship Coaching and Job rotation. OJT is the most dominant form of training in the world today not just because it is safe or economical but also because in many instances it is the only practical way of learning a job. It is a traditional and proven methodology. Numerous studies indicate that it is the most effective form of job training.

On-the-job training programmes range from formal training with one-on-one master-apprentice set-ups to learning by watching master-to-many-student arrangements. In this sense, the most formal types of on-the-job training are distinct from classroom training largely as they take place onsite where work is being performed.

The on-the-job types of training are discussed below:

1. Apprenticeship Training: It is a process by which unskilled workers become skilled workers, with the combination of formal learning and long term on-job training.

Apprenticeship training, *"means a course of training in any industry or in pursuance of a contract of apprenticeship and under prescribed terms and conditions which may be different for different categories of apprentices":* ***Directorate General of Employment and Training Ministry of Labour Government of India***

2. Informal Learning: Majority of people learn effectively through informal learning while performing their jobs on a daily basis in collaboration with their colleagues.

It can take place in any organisation. Managers do not actually arrange informal training but they make sure that it occurs. It brings good results in employees' work since it is arranged informally where workers show active interest in learning.

3. Job Instruction Training: Many jobs consist of a logical sequence of steps and are best taught in a step–by-step manner. This step-by-step process is called Job Instruction Training (JIT).

Performa of JIT

Job Instruction Training
1. Prepare a Training Timetable **Define Objectives** • Who is going to attend the training? • Training for which skill is to be given • What is the training duration? **2. Break-down of the Job** • Enlist important steps • Highlight key points and mention reasons • Make safety as a main point **3. Keep Everything Ready** • Keep all the components required for the training ready **4. Arrange the Work Area** • Arrange the work area just like actual working conditions

4. T group: It is also known as sensitivity training. It is a small group of people generally of five to seven accompanied by one or two trainers. The purpose of this training is to focus on and develop the behavioural aspects of an individual's personality. Focus is on developing decision making skills, leadership skills and group dynamics of an individual.

5. **Job Rotation:** Job rotation is the method in which an employee is moved from one job to another. This helps an employee to have a general understanding of how the organisation operates. The purpose of this method is to provide trainees with a larger organisational perspective and a greater understanding of different functional areas. However it may give rise to several problems especially when the trainees are put on various jobs at frequent intervals. In such a case, trainees do not stay in any single phase of the operation for long which is required to develop a high degree of expertise. But it generally improves participants' job skills and job satisfaction. It also provides scope to develop a network within the organisation. For the fast learners there are opportunities of promotion and higher salaries. Lateral transfers are beneficial for developing new talents.

But there are also chances of getting more workload for participants.

6. **Coaching:** It is a kind of training which is performed on a daily basis where feedback is given to employees by their immediate supervisors. It is a continuous process of learning. Supervisor explains things, answers questions and throws light on how things should be done. Coaching is very useful when an employee demonstrates a new competency or expresses interest in a different job with the same organisation. It involves observation, explanation, offering possible alternatives and follow up.

Off-the-Job Training

1. **Simulated Training:** In this type of training the trainee learns on actual equipment which they need to operate but the training is done off-the-job. It is provided when on-the-job training is costly and dangerous. It is also called as vestibule training. It is undertaken in a separate room where all the equipment is placed to provide training. It involves the use of simulators.

Simulation presents likely problem situations and decision alternatives to the trainee. For example, certain activities are simulated and the trainee will be asked to make appropriate decisions to support those activities. The results of that decision are provided with an explanation of what would have happened if the given decision was applied at the actual workplace. In this way trainee can judge the situation with the given decision. Simulation can be exercised with case study, role playing and vestibule training.

3. **Management Games:** Various leadership, motivational, analytical and decisive games are organised for employees in groups of five to six persons. Each group typically is asked to decide how much to produce, how much inventory to maintain and how much to spend on advertising etc.

Management games can be effective when participants are involved completely with their best interest. Trainees can develop their problem solving skills and focus their attention on planning.

4. **Outside Seminars:** Many companies and universities offer traditional as well as web-based classroom seminars on management development. These bring professionals from different areas ranging from accounting, finance, IT, TQM etc. and specialised seminars can be delivered.

5. University Related Programmes: Many universities provide special extension programmes to executives on leaderships, supervision, motivation etc. These can run for a week to one or two months as well. Students are generally experienced managers from various industries. Case studies and lecture methods provide the top level management with the latest management skills.

6. Role Playing: This creates a realistic situation and makes employees assume the role of a specific person in that situation. The aim is to develop trainees in various areas such as leadership, delegating and decision-making.

7. Behaviour Modelling: It includes educating on the right way of doing things and provides feedback on the trainee's performance. In this type, firstly, the trainees watch live or video example that shows the model behaving effectively in a problem situation. A video helps to know the situation more clearly. Secondly, trainees are given roles to play in a simulated situation. They practice and rehearse effective behaviours as shown in videos. And the trainer then provides detailed feedback based on the trainees' performance in a role play situation.

8. Corporate Universities: Many firms establish their in-house development centres which are also called as Corporate Universities. They typically offer a catalogue of courses and special programmes to support employees for their different corporate training needs. Web based educational portals provide added value to such corporate universities.

9. Executive Coaches: It is an outside consultant who questions the executive's boss, peers, subordinates and family in order to indentify the executive's strength and weaknesses and to counsel the executives so that he or she can capitalise on those strengths and overcome weaknesses.

10. Audio-visual Training: It includes DVD's, films, power point presentations, video conferencing and audiotapes which are very effectiveand widely used. According to recent trends trainers mostly give presentations through modern methods though it is very expensive as compared to conventional methods. But audiovisual training drags more attention of the trainees and also helps them to remember easily. Audiovisual training gives more illustration on actual troubleshooting which helps the worker in resolving problems easily.

Web Based Training

1. Computer Based Training: It is one of the interactive systems which increases employees' knowledge or skills. Many firms have developed courses for their franchisee's employees and made them available on DVDs. Interactive multimedia training integrates text, video, graphics, photos, animation and sound to produce a training environment with which the trainer interacts with the trainee.

It includes:

(a) Programmed instructions (PI): It consists of texts, graphics and multimedia that are stored in a computer's memory and are connected to one another electronically.

(b) Computer Managed Instruction (CMI): It uses a computer to manage administrative functions such as registration, record keeping, scoring, grading etc.

(c) Intelligent Tutoring System (ITS): It makes use of artificial intelligence for providing tutoring.

(d) Virtual Reality: It is the advance form of computer simulation, creating a simulated environment that is virtually same as physical environment. A trainee learns by interacting with objects in the electronic environment.

2. Electronic Performance Support System: According to **Barry Raybould,** *"An Electronic Performance Support System is a computer-based system that improves worker's productivity by providing on-the-job access to integrated information, advice and learning experiences".*

Gloria Gery defines it as *"an integrated electronic environment that is available to and easily accessible by each employee and is structured to provide immediate, individualised on-line access to the full range of information, software, guidance, advice and assistance, data, images, tools and assessment and monitoring systems; to permit job performance with minimal support and intervention by others."*

Electronic performance support systems are used for understanding the task and helps in following procedures and processes. It also gives access to knowledge where users can find information they need. Another important aspect is alternate forms of knowledge representation which may be video, audio, text, image and data.

3. Distance and Internet Based Training: Distance learning methods range from paper and pencil correspondence courses to tele-training, video-conferencing and modern Internet based courses.

Tele Training: From the central location, the trainer teaches groups of employees at remote locations. It saves time and cost on physical based training.

Video-conferencing: It allows people from one location to communicate with people from another location through necessary equipments. It involves using video cameras and different participants joining a video conference lecture room.

Various products, like Blackboard and WebCT, support online learning endeavours. For example, WebCT provides a process for delivering course content via Power Point slides. It enables learners and instructors to interact live and asynchronously via online chat rooms and discussion forums.

Internet Based Learning: It is a popular method which is demanded more than any other method. It is more effective than classroom method for teaching descriptive topics. Web based instruction and classroom instruction are equally effective for teaching procedural topics.

4. Virtual Classrooms: It is a software that enables multiple remote learners, using their PC's or laptops to participate in the video based classrooms. It enables communication with members of the training by two way audio, video and chats.

Apart from the above three methods there is programmed learning which also helps to provide training to the trainees.

Programmed Learning:

It is a systematic method for teaching job skills involving presentation of questions or facts, allowing the person to respond and give immediate feedback to the learner on the accuracy of his or her answer.

It consists of three parts:

- Presenting facts, questions, and problems to the learner.
- Allowing a person to respond.
- Providing feedback on the basis of answer.

The main advantage of programmed learning is the less amount of time involved. It also facilitates learning because it lets trainees learn at their own pace and reduces the learner's risk of error.

In order to meet the training and development needs of an organisation, various training programmes are designed from time to time. It is a continuous process. Many organizations organise their own training programmes with the help of training professionals, experts. But arrangements are also made for the employees to attend the training programmes organised by outside professional organisations.

However, there are some important considerations which are taken into consideration while designing the training programmes. They are :

(1) Area of training contents, (2) Characteristics of trainees, (3) Key learning principles, and (4) Cost of training. Let us consider each of these considerations in brief:

1. **Areas of Training Contents:** Information, acquisition of skills and abilities, decision-making skills and problem solving skills are important basic areas of training programme content and generally, training programmes include more than one of these content. The success of any training programme depends much on the identification of proper areas of training content.

2. **Characteristics of Trainees:** Characteristics of trainees is another important area of consideration which affect the choice of a training programme. While organising training programmes, the number of trainees, their abilities, skills, attitudes, needs and other such factors are required to be taken into consideration. If an organisation decides to bring about major changes in its objectives, policies, it is obvious that every employee is required to be given the training.

3. **Key Learning Principles:** Training is an organised procedure and people learn knowledge and also acquire various skills. The training is rooted in the learning process. Learning is that process by which skills, knowledge, habits, attitudes etc., are acquired and utilised by the learners in such a way so that their behaviour is modified. Training endeavours to induce learning for bringing about a relatively

permanent change in knowledge, skills, behaviour etc. Studies of human learning imply several principles which offer valuable guidance for designing training programmes. Some of the important learning principles are conditions of practice, knowledge of results, relevance of material and transfer to the job. Training programmes are expected to motivate the trainees to learn these principles and therefore, training methods selected should incorporate important key learning principles depending upon the area of training content.

4. **Cost of Training:** Cost of training is yet another consideration in designing a training programme. Budget size of a training programme depends upon the number of trainees, methods adopted for completing training programme etc. Cost-benefit analysis is done while deciding the budget of a training programme.

E- Training:

Introduction: E-training has become the need of an hour now. Many organizations follow this practice. The technology can spread across the world due to E- Training. It makes peoples learning very easy

- e-training means the delivery of learning or training programme by electronic means.

- e-training involves the use of a computer or any other electronic device to provide training or educational material.

- e-training is the convergence of the internet and learning, or Internet-enabled learning.

Importance of e-training:-

- Employees within and outside of an organization can attend training

- Due to online learning, space problems especially in the small offices becomes very easy.

- The workplaces and homes are being networked with sophisticated communication devices, thereby paving the way for information from anywhere in the world and at any time.

- Ever changing world of business. : Thus, when business cycles are shortened, organizations cannot afford to send their employees away from work for several weeks or months to undergo classroom training. Under these conditions organizations, by deploying the e-training solutions, want employees to learn and perform simultaneously.

- e-training solutions can bridge this gap by providing ready information to such distributed workforce anywhere and anytime, thereby creating an instant expertise.

- Traditional classroom training is quite expensive accommodating all employees, in to one roof requires huge space and money. E-training is better option for people sitting at home or from anywhere can learn or attend online sessions through webinars.

- Business processes and products are constantly changing, which creates the need for retraining people very often.

Types of e-training:

1. Synchronous

2. Asynchronous

Both training depends on how the learning and teaching takes place.

1. In the **synchronous approach**, both learning and teaching takes place in real time even though the trainer and learners are physically separated from each other.

Online Webinar sessions are held to conduct synchronous type of learning.

Advantages of synchronous approach learning, from anywhere without having to travel to a farther distance to reach a training center and the convenience of interacting with the trainer and other learners instantly.

The disadvantages is learner has to find time to attend the classes in keeping the appointed time and without having the option to learn whenever he wants or finds time.

2. In the **asynchronous approach**, the learning takes place with time delay as well as the trainer and learner are physically separated from each other.

The advantages, the learner not only can learn from any place of his choice but also at a time of his own convenience. The cost of asynchronous training is quite lower than synchronous training.

The disadvantages, there is no scope for an instant question-answer session and listening to the perspectives of other learners. The learner is cut-off from other learners and the trainer, at the lime of learning.

E-training process there are a sense of activities involved in the successful implementation of e-training programmes which can together be termed as e-training programme process. E-training programme process is by and Large similar to traditional training process with minor changes.

The e-training process has following stages:

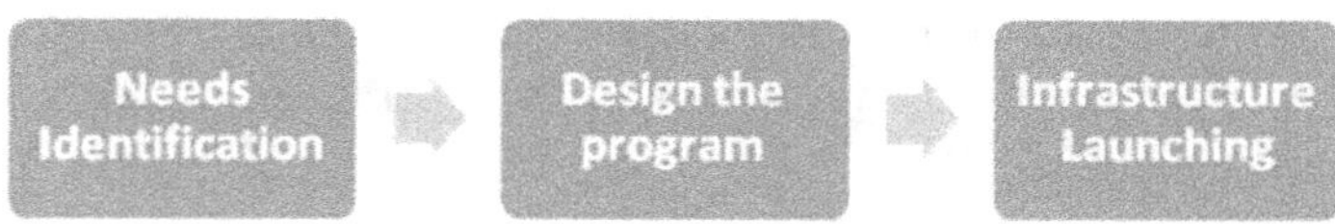

Fig. 4.3: Steps of e-training process

1. Needs Identification.

2. Design the programme.

3. Infrastructure Launching.

Needs Identification: The idea of introducing e-training should start with needs identification. Needs identification will have to look at the business case for investment in e-training as well as the need and comfort level of employees with specific reference to e-training.

Design the programme: Once a clear need is identified and the management accepts the proposal for investment to develop e-training programmes, then the training managers have to look for designing appropriate programmes based on the nature of learning as well as the characteristics of the learners.

Infrastructure: After designing the programme structure, the training managers have to create the E-training infrastructure like computers, broad band connectivity, video conferencing and other devices. Once all the development work is completed it is now time for launching the programme. A company should always start with pilot programmes to test the suitability and understand the bottlenecks, if any.

Advantages and disadvantages of e-training:

Advantages:

- Reduced cost and saved revenues

- Learning times can be reduced, an average of 40% to 60%.

- Expert knowledge is communicated, but more importantly captured, **Launching** with good e-training and knowledge management systems

- On-demand availability enables students to complete training conveniently at off-hours or from home.

- Confidence that refresher or quick refresher materials are available reduces burden of responsibility of mastery.

Disadvantages:

- **Costs Involved:** Initial cost required for e-training solution is larger due to the need for technology infrastructure and costs associated with programme development.

- **Learner capabilities:** Learner capabilities matter a lot in the e-training techniques particularly of asynchronous training. An illiterate employee cannot be expected to operate computer and the Internet for training.

- **Cultural barriers:** There are still people in this world, particularly among the working classes, who believe that use of computer and communication technology at work renders thousands of people jobless. Such unfounded beliefs may really work as stumbling blocks for the penetration of e-training across larger population.

- **Trainer Personality:** Online training demands much more openness, flexibility, concern and friendly attitude on the part of the trainer. The trainer has to compensate for the lack of physical proximity in every possible way. Hence, the delivery of learning or training program by electronic means.

- E-training involves the use of a computer or any other electronic device to provide training or educational material
- E-training is the convergence of the internet and learning, or Internet-enabled learning.

Recent Trends in E-Training:

1. Blended Training:

Blended training is an approach which combines e-training with other traditional methods of training for delivering a training solution. Blended training programmes in the corporate training world is defined as any possible combination of a wide range of training delivery approaches designed to solve specific business problems. "Blended Training" is the natural evolution of e-training into an integrated programme of multiple media types, applied toward a business problem in an optimum way. It is one of the simplest approach to create electronic content and surround it with human, interactive content.

- This approach of surrounding e-training with humans enables to create high interest accountability and real assessment of the results of the training programme.
- In order to make blended training more powerful, trainers look at all the media as options like classroom training, web-based training, webinars, CDROM courses, video, and simulations.

2. Microlearning:

Microlearning was a strong trend in times. Many organizations are increasingly looking at microlearning as an important solution. It is a great method of implementing learning in small chunks that are objective driven and can be easily and quickly deployed within organizations.

Organizations that are looking to take advantage of microlearning will continue to benefit from this interesting and innovative mode of learning.

Learners benefit too as they get through the modules quickly and can repeat the learning many times as well. Retention is better, and they are less fussy about going through a boring hour-long module.

Microlearning can be implemented as videos, small games, quizzes, and infographics.

The great advantage of microlearning is that it can be implemented on any device.

3. Social learning:

In addition to social collaborative tools, organizations are also experimenting with cross-functional project-based learning, creating online learning marketplaces and structured mentoring forums. At the very minimum, employees expect workplace technologies that allow:

- social networking,
- instant messaging,

- online collaboration,
- video conferencing.

Humans are social by nature: 87% of employees say that sharing knowledge with their team is critical for learning. 34% of organizations are already investing in social learning tools and over the next few years we anticipate the uptake will accelerate. The increasing complexity of work, rise of the contingent and freelance workforce, and the desire to work 'anywhere, anytime' will drive the adoption of social collaboration and knowledge-sharing tools.

5. Employee-curated content:

Relevant content is what matters most to employees. Employees are satisfied with the relevance of the content provided by their organisation. How can we help employees cut through the clutter? Employees want the ability to create their own online content and share learning resources. It's no surprise that peer-to-peer learning continues to gain traction – empowering people to share relevant content with their colleagues.

Organisations are also supporting apps which curate, publish and share content to keep peers, teammates and managers across the latest and most relevant content. Crowdsourcing means content is constantly refreshed, removing the barrier of irrelevant information which can deter time-poor learners.

6. Mobile (aka on-demand):

Employees expect to access content anytime, anywhere via a mobile device. Although this trend isn't new, corporate adoption levels have lagged behind employee expectations. Over three-quarters of employees do at least some of their learning on a mobile device and 99% of mobile learners believe the mobile format enhanced their learning. Despite this, mobile access is ranked as the second-largest challenge to learning from an employee's perspective. Tellingly, access to mobile learning doesn't register within the top three perceived challenges L&D professionals face. Looking to the future, 23% plan to purchase mobile learning solutions and this trend is expected to accelerate. Organisations that want to improve the learning experience of their employees need to ensure mobile is part of the solution

7. Data and analytics :

Employee training budgets have increased year after year. And they expected to trend upwards in the coming years. Executives are looking for financial returns, yet many professionals struggle to tie real-world results to talent development spend. Nearly one-third (32%) of executives say demonstrating ROI is the top challenge for the talent development team. Only 22% of people managers feel the same. So how can organisations measure and articulate the ROI of investing in learning and development? The key is to take an evidence-based approach to gathering learning insights that's based on robust data and metrics. Articulating the ROI of learning and development initiatives requires assessing an organisation's development needs, analysing the outcomes of learning, then describing how this closes development gaps to drive productivity.

8. Gamification, Augmented and Virtual Reality (AR/VR):

Although gamification has been around for a while, we expect it will continue to gain traction as more millennials enter the workforce. Current research by HR Technologist states, "Younger generations today are intimately familiar with the concept of gamification. Most of them grew up with video games and smartphones, so gamifying corporate learning can become a natural extension of learning."

Gamifying elements of learning such as compliance training gives people a 'safe' environment where they can take risks and get positive reinforcement. It also helps people see how they stack up against their peers, earn badges, collaborate and feel a sense of accomplishment.

9. People analytics:

Learning and development is not a standalone function. It has a crucial role to play in underpinning the organisation's strategic workforce vision. Forward-thinking organisations are moving beyond descriptive to predictive analytics. Learning data is increasingly being incorporated into people analytics to understand the impact of learning on things like retention and staff promotion. People analytics help organisations understand their workforce by making data about employee attributes, behaviour and performance more accessible, interpretable and actionable, according to research by Science Direct.

Distinction between Training and Development

Sr. No.	Training	Development
1.	Training is for short term.	Development is for long term.
2.	Training is imparted for skills.	Development is imparted for attitude, knowledge and beliefs.
3.	It educates on concepts of technical and mechanical nature.	It educates on concepts of philosophical and theoretical nature.
4.	It is meant for managerial and non-managerial staff.	It is meant only for managerial staff.
5.	Purpose is to give specific job related knowledge.	Purpose is to give broader knowledge.
6.	The focus is on today's needs of an organisation.	The focus is on tomorrow's needs of an organisation.
7.	It is task oriented.	It is skill oriented.

Points to Remember

- Training is a very essential component of an organisation as it improves employees' abilities and leadership skills and brings in positive attitude. Performance is drastically enhanced with the right kind of training in the right place with the right people.

- **Training** is a planned programme which is designed to improve performance, impart skills, abilities and attitude.

- **Formal Training methods include:** On-the-Job Training which covers coaching, mentoring, job rotation, apprenticeship training, and committee assignments whereas Off-the-Job training includes Case study, Role Play, lectures, conferences, simulation and programmed instructions.

- Management Development programmes are techniques of developing managers with their abilities and attitude towards the work.

- MDP has On-the-Job as well as Off-the-job training methods.

Multiple Choice Questions

1. ...... provides new employees with the basic background information required to perform their jobs satisfactorily.

    (a) Employee recruitment

    (b) Employee selection

    (c) Employee orientation

    (d) Employee development

    (e) Training

2. Orientation typically includes information on ....

    (a) employee benefits   (b) personnel policies

    (c) daily routine   (d) safety measures

    (e) all of the above

3. The methods used to give new or present employees the skills they need to perform their jobs are called ....

    (a) orientation   (b) training

    (c) development   (d) appraisal

    (e) management

4. Employers use ...... to ensure that employees are working towards organisational goals.

   (a) performance management process

   (b) employee orientation programme

   (c) management by objectives programme

   (d) rewards programme

   (e) just-in-time system

5. Which of the following has the highest influence on organisational effectiveness?

   (a) appraisal   (b) feedback

   (c) training   (d) goal-setting

   (e) technology

6. The first step in a training programme is to ......

   (a) assess the programme's successes or failures

   (b) present the programme to a small test audience

   (c) design the programme content

   (d) conduct a needs analysis

   (e) train the targeted group of employees

7. What is the second step in the training process?

   (a) assess the programme's successes or failures

   (b) present the programme to a small test audience

   (c) design the programme content

   (d) conduct a needs analysis

   (e) train the targeted group of employees

8. The third step in the training process is to ......

   (a) assess the programme's successes or failures

   (b) present the programme to a small test audience

   (c) design the programme content

   (d) conduct a needs analysis

   (e) train the targeted group of employees

9. The fourth step in the training process is to ......

   (a) assess the programme's successes or failures

   (b) present the programme to a small test audience

(c) design the programme content

(d) conduct a needs analysis

(e) train the targeted group of employees

10. What is the final step in the training process?

(a) assess the programme's successes or failures

(b) present the programme to a small test audience

(c) design the programme content

(d) conduct a needs analysis

(e) train the targeted group of employees

11. Rao is currently identifying the specific job performance skills needed by analysing the skills of prospective trainees and developing knowledge and performance objectives based on the deficiencies found. Rao is working on the ...... step in the training and development process.

(a) first	(b) second

(c) third	(d) fourth

(e) fifth

12. Which of the following is not a consideration when designing a training programme that motivates the trainees?

(a) provide the opportunity to apply the material

(b) provide prompt feedback

(c) utilise a half or three-fourths day schedule

(d) pay the trainees for the time spent in training

(e) allow trainees to set their own pace

13. Which of the following is recommended for training sessions to maximise learning?

(a) a full day	(b) a half-day

(c) one hour	(d) three hours

(e) two hours

14. If an employer fails to train an employee adequately and an employee subsequently does harm to a third party, the court could find the employer liable for ....

(a) negligent hiring	(b) discrimination

(c) negligent training	(d) occupational fraud

(e) adverse action

15. Which of the following steps will not help employers to protect themselves against charges of negligent training?

    (a) confirm employee claims of skill and experience

    (b) provide extensive training

    (c) evaluate the degree to which training lowers risks associated with job

    (d) pay employees for time spent in training

    (e) all of the above

16. Under which situation below, should an employer pay an employee for time spent in training?

    (a) the training programme is voluntary

    (b) the training programme is directly related to the trainee's job

    (c) the trainee does not perform any productive work during the programme

    (d) the training programme is conducted outside working hours

    (e) the training provides no immediate benefit to the employer

17. ...... is a detailed study of the job to determine what specific skills the job requires.

    (a) Needs analysis   (b) Task analysis

    (c) Performance analysis   (d) Training strategy

    (e) Development planning

18. Employers can supplement the job description and specification with a ...... that consolidates information regarding required tasks and skills, in a format that is helpful for determining training requirements.

    (a) performance record form

    (b) training assessment form

    (c) task analysis record form

    (d) skill sheet

    (e) work function analysis

19. A task analysis record form contains all of the following information except ......

    (a) task list

    (b) required skill set

    (c) quality of performance

    (d) employee name

    (e) performance conditions

20. Employers can identify training needs for new employees by ......

    (a) reviewing job descriptions

    (b) reviewing performance standards

    (c) performing the job

    (d) questioning current job holders

    (e) all of the above

| Answer to MCQ's |

(1) - (c),   (2) - (e),   (3) - (b),   (4) - (a),   (5) - (d),   (6) - (d),   (7) - (c),   (8) (b),   (9) - (e),
(10) - (a),   (11) - (a),   (12) - (d),   (13) - (b),   (14) - (c),   (15) - (d),   (16) - (b),
(17) - (b),   (18) - (c),   (19) - (d),   (20) - (e)

Project Questions

1. You are training someone to use SAP software in their office. Which training methods do you suggest?

2. Analyse the training programme of a heavy machinery industry. Discover the steps of training and development of their employees.

3. Design a training programme for the candidates who are going to join an Automobile Company.

Case Study

Introduction

South wood school administrators realised that a newly designed performance management system for their support staff would require a formal training programme. Designing and implementing the new performance management system was a challenge for the organisation; the last system was unpopular with employees, and negative feelings about the value of performance management linger.

Case Overview

Some of the issues identified with the previous performance management system included:

- Annual deadlines to complete the process were missed by many staff members.

- Some staff members were confused about what exactly is needed to be completed and when.

- There were complaints that the previous system was a "waste of time" and that there were no measurable outputs.

- A trade union representative felt that the system was not appropriate for all staff members.

- Criteria on the forms were irrelevant for support staff. For example, support staff could not set objectives in pupil progress or have lessons observed.

- There was little attention on identifying training needs and where needs had been identified, there was no follow-up with appropriate actions.

- Appraisals were led by teachers with little knowledge on their appraisees' jobs.

- Performance meetings were a one-way process; often, performance goals were identified before the meeting and without the appraisee's input.

Case Details

The case study consists of two parts:

I.   Designing the training programme for managers (appraisers).

II. Designing the training programme for appraisees.

I.   Designing the training Programme For managers (appraisers).

The managers in this case study are the appraisers in the new performance management process. In some cases, they will be teachers with no formal management qualifications. In other cases, they will be support staff with specific management responsibilities in the organisation.

Needs Analysis:

Initially, the director of administration recommended that a selection of managers complete a standard Internet-based training programme provided by an online training organisation. Managers who completed the online training would receive a certificate of achievement. Based on input from the HR manager, however, it was decided that a custom-designed programme would be more appropriate because it would better meet managers' needs. A custom-designed programme would also allow the school to relate the training back to their new performance management system and provide flexibility in the programme's delivery.

There were a number of options available to determine who would design and deliver the programme:

- The HR manager could design and deliver the training.

- The HR manager could design the content and the training could be conducted by a member of the school's senior management team.

- An external consultant could design and deliver the training.

- An external consultant could design the content and the HR manager could conduct the training.

In the end, it was decided that the HR manager would design and develop the programme with support from the senior management team, if necessary.

The reasons for this decision:

- **Specialised knowledge:** The HR manager had developed the new performance management system and was therefore the most knowledgeable person about it.

- **Experience:** The HR manager was experienced in developing training programmes.

- **Cost:** This was the least expensive option; no direct costs would be incurred.

- **Context:** It would be easier to include specifics about the new performance management system if the training was designed by an internal person.

- **Flexibility:** The sessions could be run at the times convenient to managers, which may have been more difficult to accommodate with an external trainer.

Designing the Training:

A focus group discussion was held with five managers, to find out what they wanted from the training and to assess their concerns about performance management. This was a useful process. The managers wanted to include training on how to deal with difficult people, which otherwise may not have been included in the programme. Including this also assured managers that their views were important and had been considered in the programme's design.

The training would take place in-house and outside the normal workday. It was agreed that the most appropriate method was a two-hour workshop. The workshop would include various activities geared to develop the skills and knowledge of the participants:

- Trainer-led interactive presentations.

- Role play exercises.

- Use of a specially designed case study.

Questions:

1. Analyse the case and give a suitable title.

2. Define the problem area and solve with the right approach.

Questions for Discussion

1. State Benefits of Employee Training and also explain Training Methods.
2. What is Training and Development? Describe Off-the-Job Training Methods.
3. Discuss Need and Objectives of Training Programmes. How Training Programmes are Evaluated?

4. State the Need and Objectives of Training.

5. Write Short Notes:

    (a) On-the-Job Training.

    (b) Objectives of Training.

6. Discuss briefly Important Methods of Training of Personnel.

✍ ✍ ✍

ORGANIZATIONAL BEHAVIOUR AND HUMAN RESOURCE MANAGEMENT

BBA (Computer Application) Sem. II

MODEL QUESTION PAPER

(CBCS 2019 Pattern)

Time : 3 Hours   **Maximum Marks : 70**

Instructions to the candidates :

    (i)   Question No. 1 and Question No. 8 are compulsory.

    (ii)   Attempt any 4 questions from Q.2 to Q. 7.

    (iii) Figures to the Right Indicate the full marks.

Q. 1 : (A) Fill in the Blanks with correct Alternatives :   **[5]**

    1.   .... means the study of the behaviour of individuals and groups in the organisations.

        (a) HRM   (b) HRP

        (c) OB   (d) HRD

    2.   .... model of OB is an extension of the Supportive model of OB.

        (a) Autocratic   (b) The Supportive

        (c) The System   (d) Collegial

    3.   HRM is ______

        (a) employee oriented   (b) employer oriented

        (c) legally oriented   (d) none of the above

    4.   HRM is ______

        (a) a staff function   (b) a line function

        (c) a staff function, line function and accounting function

        (d) all of the above

    5.   Recruitment policy usually highlights need for establishing ______

        (a) job specification   (b) job analysis

        (c) job description   (d) none of the above

Ans. :   **(1) - (c), (2) - (d), (3) - (a), (4) - (a), (5) - (a).**

(B) State True or False   **[5]**

    1.   Human Resource Planning is also known as 'Manpower Planning'.

    2.   Promotion is an external source of recruitment.

    3.   HRM is a comprehensive function.

    4.   Training is a planned, organised and controlled activity.

    5.   Training helps to remove defects in the process of selection.

Ans. :   **(1) - (True), (2) - (False), (3) - (True), (4) - (True),**

              (5) - (True).

Q. 2 : Explain the various models of Organisational Behaviour.   **[10]**

Q. 3 : State the scope and functions of HRM.   **[10]**

Q. 4 : Explain the various external sources of Recruitment.   **[10]**

Q. 5 : Describe the Process of Selection.   **[10]**

Q. 6 : Explain the various Methods of Training.   **[10]**

Q. 7 : What is HRP ? State its Merits and Demerits   **[10]**

Q. 8 : Write Short Notes (Attempt Any Four) .   **[20]**

    1. Quality of Work Life.

    2. Cultural Diversity.

    3. Role of HR Manager.

    4. E-recruitment.

    5. Types of Interview.

    6. Recent Trends in Training.